On Presence

BY THE SAME AUTHOR

Existentialism: A Theory of Man
The Sleeping Beauty
    2d ed., Nostalgia: An Existential Exploration of
        Longing and Fulfillment in the Modern Age
    3d ed., The Sleeping Beauty and Other Essays
The Seventh Solitude: Metaphysical Homelessness
        in Kierkegaard, Dostoevsky, and Nietzsche
Human Love: Existential and Mystical
The Path of Darkness
The World of the Thriller
The Existential Experience
Journey from Paradise: Mt. Athos and the Interior
        Life

On Presence

VARIATIONS AND REFLECTIONS

RALPH HARPER

TRINITY PRESS INTERNATIONAL
PHILADELPHIA

First Published 1991

Trinity Press International
3725 Chestnut Street
Philadelphia, PA 19104

Interior design and production by Publishers' WorkGroup
Cover design by Steven Zellers

Library of Congress Cataloging-in-Publication Data

Harper, Ralph.
  On presence : variations and reflections / Ralph Harper.
    p.   cm.
  Includes bibliographical references.
  ISBN 1-56338-005-6 (pbk.)
  1. Ontology. 2. Presence of God. 3. Mysticism. 4. Proust,
  Marcel, 1871-1922. I. Title.
  BD331.H3165 1991
  110--dc20   90-24283
                                  CIP

92   93   94   95   96   6   5   4   3   2

Contents

A Note to the Reader   vii

Introduction   1

1. **Anonymous Presence**   9

    Anonymous Presence   9
    Access to Being   12
    Presence Refracted   16
    Postscript   18

2. **Being as Presence**   21

    Being as Presence   21
    Reality Has Deceived Me   25
    Invasions of Being: 31
       A Whole Secret System of Life   31
       A World of Dreams   32
    Postscript   35

3. **Presence and Mystery**   39

    Presence and Mystery   39
    Presence: In Te, Domine, Speravi   45
    Mystery: 47
       Theophanies   47
       Ordinary Mysteries and Obscure Pleasures   48
    Postscript   51

4. Mystical Presence   55

Mystical Presence   55
Metaphysical Desire   61
The Ideal of Unsatisfied Desire   65
The Power of Fantasy   67
Postscript   69

5. Presence as Glory   73

Presence as Glory   73
The Glory of Hawthorns   79
Exhilaration in Autumn   82
Postscript   85

6. Living Presence   89

Living Presence   89
Withdrawal from Life: 93
    A Lost Eurydice   94
    Dreams of a Traveller   96
    Final Crossroads   98
Postscript   100

7. Real Presence   105

Real Presence   105
Salve Regina   108
Viaticum   111
Postscript   115

8. A Secret Understanding   119

A Final Unscientific Postscript   125

Selected Bibliography   129

A Note to the Reader

The world is full of presence. Presences linger, make a difference, have authority. It is hard to imagine what the world would be like if we had to deny presence. We would have to become reconciled to living in a world of almost total incoherence. That is not how most people live.

I myself have lived on the fringes of both church and university, and have been fortunate in escaping the deep skepticisms affirmed by "the current masters of emptiness."[1] From logical positivism and language philosophy to analytical philosophy and deconstructionism, much of the intellectual practice of our century has been inhibited by doctrinaire skepticisms as arrogant and intolerant as any religious or political mindset.

We are sometimes told that there is really no such thing as personal identity or continuity. My own fifty years of intellectual continuity is not, I would suppose, the only exception to such a dogma. The heart of personal continuity is memory of presence: self, other people, places, art, nature, and the ability to make promises and keep them. We cannot do without these presences: it is "the holiness of the particular"[2] that makes life worth living, its numinous mystery, its power to change us.

We need not go about looking for final meanings. There is always something else to see and say. The absolutes and final meanings that skeptics set up as straw men to destroy do not figure in everyday life for most of us. Even if we think of our lives in terms of longing—and I always have—it is more likely to be a longing for presence discovered or presence recovered than for some big truth.

We are not obliged by an agreed epistemology (indeed, there is none) to postulate a last word. In any event, disappointment need not be the last word in life or knowledge. There is always the possibility (faint though it may be) of reversal of fate or further insight in understanding. I have been especially enlightened by Proust who disclaimed the possibility of presence and yet dreamed of presence so vividly that he enabled others to believe in what he himself denied.

We have too short a time on this earth to pass up any chance to find words and images to live by. I believe almost everyone is capable of being moved by some person, place, nature or individual work of art. Of course, there is instability and incoherence in and about us all the time. There is also an inexhaustible store of Being to keep us permanently in awe.

i

After finishing this book, and before writing this Note, I thought for a while that it might have something in common with Rudolf Otto's *The Idea of the Holy*. But presence is not just an idea—nor, for that matter, is the holy—and because it is an idea now under attack in some academic circles in France, Great Britain, and the United States, it seemed better to avoid a structural analysis and instead to attempt an exercise in remembrance. I should like what I have done here to be thought of in musical terms, as variations on a theme. Nor is this book an exercise in the history of ideas, because, properly speaking, there is no history of presence, no chronological development that I am aware of. All variations can appear at the same time and always have. And so I offer metaphysical, theological, psychological, and literary manifestations of the phenomenon of presence. My method is to record the range of presence, by way of the metaphysics (mainly theological) of Karl Rahner, the metaphysics (mainly ontological) of Louis Lavelle and Martin Heidegger, the metaphysics (mainly psychological) of Martin Buber, Gabriel Marcel, and Joseph Maréchal, by way of Gershom Scholem's psychology of the Kabbala, through the mysticism of

John of the Cross and Teresa of Avila, through the biblical story of the phenomenon of glory, side by side with Gerard Manley Hopkins' praise of glory, through the reverse, dark side of presence in Dostoevsky, through the intimations of presence in Proust, and finally by way of some observations on Christian liturgical theology.

This range of manifestations of one phenomenon—which some say does not exist—has several features in common, as readers will see for themselves, too many to make it useful to contrive a definition of presence. It is more persuasive, I think, to show rather than argue. Besides, I do not have a cause to argue, just a world to expose. More, much more, remains to be said that I have not said or thought of. I hope that readers will feel like saying now and again, "Yes, that's the way it is." My appeal is to the reflective, even the meditative man or woman who has a lively sense of the inner life and an abiding respect for the world outside his or her own mind.

I do not pretend to be offering a metaphysics of presence, even though there may seem to be suggestions here and there of a metaphysics. Even Heidegger did not do that, although I think he once hoped to. What he did was meditate on the idea of presence, and that is quite different. Until recently there has not been a metaphysics of Being as presence, not even an idea of it, whether in Plato or Aristotle, Aquinas or Hegel. In the past, presence was a religious and personal theme above all, not a theme for philosophy. But today, at a time when presence is dogmatically denied by some philosophers and literary critics, there is a wealth of example and speculation to draw on. This is, therefore, the right time to try to write seriously about presence.

ii

I wrote this book before the publication of George Steiner's *Real Presences*, a moving, Protean essay with which I am in complete agreement. Some readers may see my own essay as a complement to his, not only because my focus is on the defining features of the phenomenon of presence, but because the presences I mention are existential rather than artistic. For me, Steiner's book is a ringing confirmation, from within the academy, of my own conviction about the perils of the skepticisms that have held back too much of the intellectual order of our century. And if Steiner is read for nothing else, I hope it will be for his eloquent statements on the function of music (and its mysteries) as the most accessible source of metaphysics and "unwritten theology,"[3] a view shared by Proust.

Wittgenstein misled many when he prescribed silence over matters that he himself felt he could not speak clearly about, matters of life and death that he acknowledged to be the most important matters of all. When these are removed from philosophy, philosophy looks pretty trivial. I, on the other hand, think we have an obligation to try to say as clearly as we can what we feel really matters. Then, those who hear us with some sympathy, can take up the task where we leave off.

NOTES

1. Steiner, *Real Presences*, 135.
2. Steiner, *Real Presences*, 106.
3. Steiner, *Real Presences*, 218.

Introduction

Søren Kierkegaard and Martin Heidegger said that philosophers and theologians had forgotten the meaning of both existence and being. "It is the misfortune of our age that it has too much knowledge, that it has forgotten what it means to exist, and what inwardness signifies,"[1] said Kierkegaard, who went on, "Inwardness is subjectivity, subjectivity is passion, and an infinite, personal passionate interest in one's eternal happiness."[2] With this, existential thinking as we know it, began. A hundred years later, Heidegger began his contribution to twentieth-century philosophy by asking, "Do we in our time have an answer to the question of what we really mean by the word being? Not at all."[3] And so began a fresh approach to metaphysics as well. For the Kierkegaardian man of passionate inwardness was the same man who has an innate capacity to know being. Heidegger took his time answering his own question, and when he did, he affirmed very simply that being is presence.

It is now our turn to confess that we too no longer know what presence means.

Once mankind knew a great deal about presence. It is central to an understanding of biblical and mystical experience: the experience of meeting the hidden God. It is, therefore, curious that Heidegger never once exposed his familiarity with the Bible or with Christian mysticism, particularly Meister Eckhart. And except for one mention of love and presence, he never wrote of presence as a phenomenon of personal experience.

1

On a parallel track and at the same time, Gabriel Marcel also affirmed the metaphysical authority of presence. And yet he too never wrote of it as a theme of Christian experience.

I have always thought that Martin Buber's I-You was shorthand for a doctrine of presence. But he wrote too lyrically and at the same time too matter of factly, to suggest the terrifying theophanies of the patriarchs (which he himself resembled) or the excitations of the Hasidic ecstatics. I am sure the I-You lay behind the *disponibilité* of Marcel. Buber's emphasis on encounter, grace, wonder, and reciprocity probably set the course for Marcel's informal discussion of presence. *Presence* is to be found throughout *I and Thou*, as relation between persons, a continuum of address and response that gives meaning to life. I-You does not come across in Buber's writings with a crash of cymbals, and it is easy to underestimate Buber's depth of feeling.

No one has done more than Karl Jaspers and Karl Barth (both in 1919) to make us think about our basic insecurities, which Jaspers called "boundary-situations" (death, chance, guilt, suffering, strife), and Barth, "insecuritas." But Jaspers' lifelong preoccupation with the metaphysics of transcendence, Barth's thunder about the Wholly Other, the Divine Incognito, may have distracted even their followers from thinking about the ideal of presence that our insecurities so concretely cry out for. Once Jaspers, in a throwaway line, said something that should have led him on into the world of presence: "A look at the beloved is like a look at Being itself."[4] In this line he combined both faces of presence, the psychological and ontological.

Passion and love aside, anyone who thinks about the possibility of immediacy in knowing should be able to see the hazards of life that block one's rudimentary sense of identity, the danger of being overwhelmed by life's insecurities. Boundary-situations too have force and authority, and something in the human spirit pleads for counterparts in presence.

Presence is not dead, even if it survives for some of us only as rumors from the past. The Bible says such and such, the mystics this and that. There are moments, when we are reading, when we wonder, "Could there still be presence, alive, appealing, satisfying?" Not so long ago, William James and others tried to investigate the legitimacy of mystical experience, and, like John of the Cross and

Teresa of Avila, believed that the problem was to distinguish between illusion and reality. At least they took these witnesses seriously.

Today we are likely to be as skeptical of nonmystical presence, perhaps more so. In many forms the intellectuals of our time share Proust's skepticism that "man is the creature who cannot escape from himself,"[5] and they share his feeling that there can be no true immediacy in our knowledge of reality. One might think that at a time when so much is written about intimacy and sexuality, there might be a question at least whether intimacy might verify the possibility of the presence of persons who have force and authority.

When I was a student at Oxford in the late 1930s, even the logical positivists sometimes talked about the possibility of metaphysics. Today we ought to be talking about the possibility of presence. But the chasm widens every year between the evidence of everyday experience of each other, and what the Bible and the mystics took for granted, or for that matter, what Emily Bronte and Dostoevsky took for granted.

Perhaps men and women in the latter part of the twentieth century do not see God face to face any more; perhaps there is not, for some of us, any sure way to verify intimacy with anyone at all. I find that very difficult to accept. I have sat by dying friends, and know what it is like to participate in another person's life as it ebbs. I cannot forget the direct appeal in the eyes of those persons or convince myself that our presence to each other did not have immediacy, force, and authority. We experienced a fragment of time, a *now*. This, I believe, is something of what the Hindu *advaita* means: an experience of nonduality, such as some say they feel in sexual intimacy, a dissolving of barriers. Even Proust admitted, in a letter to a friend, that he knew that "shared loves" exist even if he had none himself.

But unhappy experiences of isolation sometimes turn people away from listening with open minds to the experiences of anyone else. Perhaps this has been taking place on a historical scale. We may have become deconditioned from being able to think about Being or presence. Heidegger thought so. The East also accuses the West of having been corrupted by specious dualisms. A subject-object habit of thinking about knowledge may not always have seemed normal.

We could do worse than to reread Meister Eckhart—whom Ananda Coomaraswamy once called the last great philosopher of the West—in order to find a thinker who takes it for granted that the mind is always present to itself. We are so used to expecting presence, if we admit it at all, to come from outside ourselves. The truth is that we are always giving ourselves to ourselves.

I know that this is casual talk about something both delicate and elusive. I fear the hardening effect of definitions and analysis at a time when we have lost the familiarity with presence both in religion and ordinary experience. I feel strongly that we must approach presence tentatively, historically, even lyrically, so that we may have a real chance to revive an intellectual climate in which serious discussion can take place. I am somewhat appalled that I seem to be the first in our time even to try.

i

There are several different ways of thinking about presence, and each can suggest the completeness of this phenomenon. The most accessible are intimacy between persons, the miracle of giving and receiving, the lingering effects of parting, even in death. It does not matter where one begins, although I will myself begin with what will seem most abstract although the most intimate of all, the presence of ourselves with ourselves. All presence has authority, a force and radiance, unreserved and yet unpredictable. One whose presence makes others come alive is one who is alive and real. Real life has its marks: immediacy, fullness, and something like the annulment of time.

I have written on this before, in *The Sleeping Beauty* and *The Existential Experience* and in "The Return Journey," an essay on some ontological theses. Each time I talked about "marks" of presence: time present, giving, mystery, grace, intimacy, totality. I said that presence is central to one trying to find an exit from boundary-situations. I thought of presence as the ideal resting place for insecurities and nostalgia. But I warned that presence was "like a sea anemone, it closes when handled."[6] I acknowledged that the sense of liberation felt around a presence is a saving grace, shared by Eastern and Western spiritualities, that presence is an experience of oneness in the middle of the fragmentation that is the curse of modern consciousness.

Most recently I have had occasion to look for examples of presence in twentieth-century literature, and have become impressed by the curious witness of Proust, who was one of the most vocal skeptics about its possibility. There are no extremes of presence in his fiction, nothing biblical or mystical as such. It is just the ordinariness of some of the scenes and dreams he records that linger longest. I think he told more than he knew he knew. For he himself and his characters lived constantly on the threshold of presence. In reading him we come to realize that however ordinary we think our lives, they are always being lived on the threshold of something mysterious. Dreams and nightmares, recollections of the countryside, the anguish and the satisfactions of life—how different they are—have the power to provoke speculation and evoke reality. When one reads Proust, the mind is led beyond Proust's own skepticism to think about the future, the quality and purpose of living. Is this not what one would expect from an experience of immediacy, an experience of time stopped?

Proust did not know the ecstasies of Teresa of Avila or Mechthild of Magdeburg, or the dark contemplation of John of the Cross. He had never had an encounter with the Divine Incognito. He denied—believe him if you can—that he was capable of an I-You relationship. But he knew as much about intimacy as anyone, deny it though he did. He never advanced new ideas about the ontological or the mystical. He did not even use the word mystery as often as his translators did. He did not characterize much; he simply told stories. That is why what he does show tells more than he himself intended or knew. An open-minded reading—itself an example of presence—can have enormous rewards. Proust does not need to promise a ride to the stars. That is for the Bible, and for Dostoevsky and Gerard Manley Hopkins. He has something safer to tender, time off with ourselves.

ii

To read Proust you have to get used to his way of alternating reflection with story, story with reflection. I intend to do the same.

I will make use of some of Proust's stories when I do. They have the same authority for many of us in this century that Holy Scripture had in earlier times. He himself begins by saying that he will tell a story which had been told him "of a love affair in which Swann had been involved before he was born, with a precision of detail which it is often easier to obtain for the lives of other people who have been dead for centuries than for those of our own most intimate friends."[7] I believe that Proust's stories can be exemplary for us, all the more because he would have been skeptical of the use to which I myself will be putting them.

The idea of presence is difficult to write about because the experience of presence is itself elusive. That is why I will match philosophical discussion with literary illustration, and then return from story to statement in an informal postscript. I want the edges to be left a bit shadowy.

Like everyone else I have certain preferences, even certain passions. I have a passion for presence, a nostalgia for presence. I am also one who is not sure that those who say they have no sense of mystery in their inner lives can make much of a connection with Proust any more than with the Bible or the mystics. But I admit I do not know the points of access to presence in other people.

What do I mean by presence? I can say this. When I am moved by a painting or by music, by clouds passing in a clear night sky, by the soughing of pines in early spring, I feel the distance between me and art and nature dissolve to some degree, and I feel at ease. I then feel that there is, briefly, no past and no future, and I am content. I feel that what I know makes me more myself than I knew before, or as Cathy says to Heathcliff, "more myself than I am."[8] And when I think of someone I really care for, I feel an exchange of understanding and acceptance that is the measure of love. This is how the saints felt about God, and I see in my own experience elements that I share with the saints and prophets, the philosophers and priests.

When I think of presence, I think of what it is like for the soul to be touched, the mystery of the whole self, body and spirit. I think of the love that wants to "banish all contradictions, banish the duality of body and soul, banish perhaps even time."[9] This is the aim of tantric maithuna. If not union, it is an as-if union. "He is always in my mind, as my own being,"[10] said Cathy of Heathcliff. It is an identity of common feeling and common understanding.

From theophanies to erotic closeness, presence feels the same, even if the personalities are not the same. Presence can be explosive, liberating, revealing, quieting. Presence has force and authority. It is the all-but union of James Joyce, the *advaya* of Hinduism, the *coincidentia oppositorum* of Nicholas of Cusa. It is not monism or dualism; it is a unitary experience and an experience of totality in the midst of shattering differences. It is the only experience that we can dream of and aspire to that might make it possible for us to live untouched at the core by violence and separation, without losing our minds or our souls.

NOTES

1. Kierkegaard, *Concluding Unscientific Postscript*, 240.
2. Kierkegaard, *Concluding Unscientific Postscript*, 33.
3. Heidegger, *Being and Time*, i.
4. Jaspers, *Philosophy*, 65.
5. Proust, III, 459.
6. Harper, *The Existential Experience*, 122.
7. Proust, I, 203.
8. Bronte, *Wuthering Heights*, 121.
9. Kundera, *The Unbearable Lightness of Being*, 54.
10. Bronte, *Wuthering Heights*, 122.

1 Anonymous Presence

Anonymous Presence

Presence is the most fundamental, although usually subliminal, experience of reality. So near, so close to our inner being and the being of all that encompasses us, it is extraordinarily difficult to apprehend in its pure state. Our sense perceptions register singularities, and we miss the underlying awareness, the base line of our acceptance of the real. The mind has to play tricks with itself to force its attention into an original awareness of Being. But it can be done. It is an ontological exercise that has much in common with the efforts of the Hindu mind to recover the initial unity of reality. If it seems different, it is mainly because the West has lost what the medieval philosophers called the intuition of Being.

Presence can, however, be intuited at all times, even if most of the time it is not even acknowledged. This is the first problem. But I would go further and affirm that presence is actually intuited at all times, subliminally. It is omnipresent. But having lost the capacity for constant wonder that anything at all exists, and having then taken for granted that what we perceive is most real, we feel free to forget the underlying sense of Being and focus on discriminating instances of Being. Somehow we must recover the initial awareness of Being, bathing consciousness in its reassuring embrace. This we can do; techniques of meditation in West and East guarantee it.

Of all the philosophers who have tried to recover a sense of Being, Meister Eckhart above all has left his distinctive mark on

Western thought. From an Eastern point of view, it is easy to understand why. Eckhart was the only Western philosopher, until the twentieth century, to share the Hindu obsession with the oneness of reality. His distinction between the Godhead and the veils of God (Being, Truth, Goodness, God), his preoccupation with the *ground of being*, have had a subliminal influence of their own on Western mysticism and metaphysics. But Eckhart was never given his due. The Church condemned him and has never exonerated him. Philosophy took the easier and shorter path of dualistic epistemology. Today we all take for granted the separateness of knower and known, subject and object, and agonize over problems of our own making. We are still embarrassed by talk of Being and by the metaphysicians who use the word.

In the present century four philosophers, all influenced by Eckhart, have revived his approach to Being. They are Martin Heidegger, Louis Lavelle, Paul Tillich, and Karl Rahner. The last two were also theologians, one Protestant, the other Catholic. Perhaps Rahner more than the others has done more to expand the spirit of Eckhart.

All four of these philosophers seem at times to speak of God and Being interchangeably. Their metaphysical instincts were so strong that they found it harder than Eckhart to remember that Being is itself a veil of the Godhead. Beyond saying that I know there is a problem here, it is sufficient for a study of presence only to acknowledge the preoccupation of all four philosophers with the mind's subliminal access to both Being and God, in the presence of whom we live. Heidegger avoided talking about God most of the time, feeling safer talking about Being, the veil of God. Tillich distinguished between the God of biblical religion and Ultimate Reality. Rahner used a safer Eckhartian approach, affirming God as the Ground of Being, for he wished to persuade his hearers that there is a subliminal, an original, orientation to both Being and God. He kept repeating that the human mind has a "pre-apprehension of Being," "a silent and uncontrollable infinity of reality is always present as mystery," "a mystery which constantly reveals itself and constantly conceals itself."[1] A variation of this: "an ontologically silent horizon of every intelligible and spatial encounter with realities."[2] Silent, horizon, intelligible, spatial, orientation, original, pre-apprehension, mystery—one can feel the desperation in the philosopher's mind as he reaches out for another word to say what he feels. The original, the subliminally original experience we have of reality is an "unthematic and anonymous knowledge"[3] of Being, of God.

Before Rahner, Louis Lavelle had already written about presence as "the initial experience."[4] Rahner, who had probably read Lavelle, expanded this into "an original orientation towards absolute mystery," our "original experience of transcendence."[5] But because it is so much a part of the subliminal awareness, it is also an experience of the immanence of Being. I realize that when one has to speak of the oneness of opposites like immanence and transcendence, one is stretching modern credulousness to the breaking point. I find it as difficult to speak of Being and transcendence as the next person. The only oneness that is even casually acceptable today is the oneness of dubious experiences of chemically induced states of cosmic awareness. But that is all the more reason for asking whether there is not something here we may have missed, which Rahner called "ultimate intimacy"[6] and Lavelle "original intimacy."[7] There are too many intellectually respectable witnesses in both West and East to an original experience of Being to brush it aside lightly. One measure of Rahner's own desperation is his use of the term "self-communication" to describe the closeness of Being and God. He says that God communicates himself to our minds through this subliminal awareness. We are aware of Being and God because Being and God are so close to us that they communicate their presence to us.

Eckhart must have been one of the oddest preachers that the pious have had to listen to. He needed to try out his insights so badly that he said such things on occasion as, "If I could not talk to you today, I would talk to the alms box."[8] He was convinced that the human mind can "pierce through to all the corners of Deity."[9] Although we can say that Eckhart had a higher conception of the power of the mind than most of us today, the real source of his influence lay in his intuitive conviction of the omnipresence of Being, and especially of an interior sense of our own presence to ourselves. "God is more intimately present to all creatures than the creature to itself. He is in the innermost depths of the soul. My truest I is God. Nothing is nearer to the soul than God; nothing is more remote from God than the creature."[10] "The eye with which I see God is the same as the eye with which God sees me."[11]

I am dealing with two elementary metaphysical questions. How close are we to being? Eckhart, Lavelle, Rahner answer: the closeness of intimate relations. What are our modes of access to Being? My own answer is: through sense and presence.

Access to Being

We do not see ourselves except in mirrors on the wall or mirrors of other people's eyes. And yet, if Eckhart and Rahner are right, we feel our being all the time subliminally. Are there then no easier ways to access? Is there no possibility of being startled into an awareness of being? In other words, could it be that there are two kinds of intuition, one that is subliminal and always present, and one that comes as a flash of insight, unasked, unsought?

To retreat back into inner space—which is what we would try to do when we make an effort to withdraw from the rush and hurry of time—is not impossible, but it requires more concentration than most of us are capable of. And we have to try to ignore the constant demands of our senses to pay attention to what they are reporting. The mystics spoke of distractions which the mind has to deal with if it is to recollect itself in order to think of God. Nonmystics as most of us are, we too must recollect, gather up what has been scattered, in order to see what is most important or most real. Proust thought about this problem longer than most, and he became convinced that recollection takes place not by means of voluntary exercises but by involuntary shocks. More than that, the shocks are administered by the very faculty of sense perception that normally gives us so much trouble, so many distractions.

This is a paradox we must face. If you despair of bringing to the surface the content of your original, subliminal experience of Being, hold on until the very thing that has inhibited you, sense perception, in its own random course makes a surprise gift of a breakthrough with something you recognize as ultimate. The tasting of the madeleine and tea by the Proustian narrator is more than another sense perception; it is an unexpected breakthrough, by way of recollection, into the lost but long loved world of childhood, the world of Combray. And the grown man, whose mind suddenly spans the time between the peal of the bell at the garden gate as Swann enters and as Swann leaves, feels as if all his life is gathered together in memory to be treasured as the only paradisal experience he is capable of. By way of the communion of tea and madeleine, communion of Proust with his mother in Paris, of Proust's narrator as a child with his Aunt Léonie in Combray, the mind practices a sacrament of entrance into "the abyss of uncertainty,"[12] "the dark region through which it must go seeking,"[13] "the vast structure of recollection."[14]

The mind is a traveller waiting for the train to paradise to start. We are only passengers and cannot control the journey. That is the message of both subliminal experience and the intuitive flashes of sense perception. I would not claim—Proust comes close to doing so—that by means of intuitive flashes the mind can have the same pure experience of Being that is our original experience. Because the flashes come by way of sense perception—taste, smell, sound, sight, touch—Being and actualities are inextricably mixed. Both are part of the inner world of space and time, that is, of space without separation, of time without regret. We do not suddenly apprehend Being; we recollect the being that we have loved and lost. And for most of us that is more than enough; we do not feel something is still missing. Proust himself referred to the nature of these intuitive experiences in two ways: first, they seem to have what is usually missing in our thinking of reality, "the idea of existence,"[15] and, second, they seem to represent the liberation of the "permanent and habitually concealed essence of things."[16] Perhaps Proust was more metaphysically inclined than I am; I admit to feeling uncomfortable with "essence of things." It has a Platonic ring that contradicts the vibrant sensuousness of the intuitions. But that is a minor disagreement, compared to the gain achieved by my conviction that by means of such intuitions the mind attains a similitude of presence.

The kind of presence recollected in intuitive flashes is by no means as pure, as simple, as fundamental as the subliminal awareness of Being. But it is so vastly different from the dualistic registration of reality as objects outside us to be numbered and named. In both cases presence comes unannounced, namelessly. What we do with presence when it arrives is quite another matter.

Proust likens the action of these flashes, metaphoric memory, to the steeping of Japanese paper flowers in water, and their magical transformation into flowers, houses, or people. He speaks more directly of those transformations as "starting-points, foundation stones for the structure of a true life."[17] "Let a noise or a scent, once heard or once smelt, be heard or smelt again, in the present and at the same time in the past, real without being actual, ideal without being abstract, and immediately the permanent and habitually concealed essence of things is liberated and our own true self which seemed to be dead is awakened."[18] An apparently random sensation becomes the link—the metaphor—between present and past, not only between similar moments but by means of the moments to the totality of the past. So the taste of the madeleine in tea revives a vision of "all the flowers in our garden and in M. Swann's park, and the waterlilies on the Vivonne and the good folk of the village and their little dwellings and the parish church and the whole of Combray and its surroundings."[19] Note the emphasis on the totality of the recollection. It is not only the idea of existence that is missing in normal perception, it is the totality. Subliminally, we take in reality and totality; consciously, we think names and numbers and take Being and its fullness for granted. Intuitively only, whether subliminally or by recollected flashes, the mind begins with existence and totality and only then moves to names and numbers.

With a kind of magic the past is recaptured and, with it, access to whatever each of us truly considers the truth. Proust understood that something special happens in such moments. That is why he insists that we notice our "special pleasure,"[20] "unreasoning pleasure,"[21] and the joy of acknowledging "some definite spiritual reality."[22] He always uses pseudo-metaphysical language of this kind when he wants to show how different such experiences are from the usual run of the conscious mind. He knows that this is the opposite of the abstract truth which he so masterfully displays in reflective passages that alternate with the narrative. We have the "illusion of a sort of fecundity."[23] He never goes quite as far as Wordsworth, as to speak of "a presence that disturbs me."[24] Proust's language is often metaphysical—the metaphysics of idealism—but not his mind. He may speak platonically, but he thinks sensually. And yet I cannot imagine him feeling at all sympathetic toward such words as "original intimacy" or "ultimate intimacy."

And yet Proust did know a sort of metaphysical intimacy within the mind, inner time and inner space. He needed a different language to distinguish between the mystery of his intuitions and recollections, and ordinary awareness. He understood quite as well as a religious novelist like Georges Bernanos that the purpose of life should not be the pursuit of happiness but the finding of joy, "a thing I would never forget, but would it ever be attainable to me?"[25] If joy is the gift of the Church, as Bernanos believed, then joy is also the gift of ontological intuition. It is attainable. Along with Proust, I think it is.

Scattered throughout the great Proustian narrative are many allusions to sense impressions that Proust thought of as starting points of deep reflection: a cloud, a triangle, a church spire, a flower, a stone, and a ray of sunlight on a roof or on a balcony, or on a stone, the level ray of a setting sun, a roof, a sound of a bell, the smell of a path, uneven paving stones, a spoon against a plate, a whiff of smoke, a cool smell of a forest background, wild grass. In only a few of these can we recognize the context in the life of the narrator. It does not matter. That is not the point of introducing them to us, or of their appearance in actual life. Granted that each impression so suddenly rendered is like "the simplest act or gesture, immured within a thousand sealed vessels."[26] We know this is a shorthand known to Proust and intelligible to anyone else only as illustrations of the kind of experience that initiated a course of recollection. Incidentally, in Proust, these moments liberate only joy, never anguish.

I have been speaking so far only of short, sharp recollections, not the more dramatic episodes which have a more complex message, such as "The Steeples of Martinville" or "Sunrise on the Train" or "A Lost Eurydice." But they too have the effect of opening doors to the soul. The difference is that the longer and more dramatic episodes direct us more openly to the totality of a life, its intricacy as well as its radiance, whereas the momentary flashes of sense perception give us only a glimpse of paradise from afar. Both are saving experiences. "It is sometimes just at the moment when we think that everything is lost that the intimation arrives which may save us; one has knocked at all the doors which lead nowhere, and then one stumbles without knowing it on the only door through which one can enter—which one might have sought in vain for a hundred years—and it opens of its own accord."[27] The entrance is along "the path you read about in books, the old lane choked in undergrowth whose entrance the weary prince could not discover."[28] It is like the door before the Law in Kafka's *The Trial* which is meant for one person only, but unlike that door it is never closed. Proust's skepticism never reached the darkness of Kafka's pessimism. Kafka may have dreamed of a world he could not believe in. I think Proust's mind actually dwelt on the threshold of that world. There is an intuitive magic that can open doors and let one at least see through into paradise, even if one cannot live there. It would be like opening the door of the wardrobe and seeing the fields of Narnia[29] but being gently prevented from going further. In Proust, one meets a curious combination of inhibition and satisfaction, of skepticism and joy. That is the sign of a pre-metaphysical mind. In the world of presence there is always some trace of absence. It is what makes us fully human. Perhaps the grand purpose of subliminal knowledge of Being is largely aspiration anyway.

Presence Refracted

Some of Henry James' stories were inspired by fragments of overheard conversations. A line or two, unfinished, out of context, was all he needed to imagine plot and characters, a fiction of his own making. If he heard too much he could not create. So it is with presence. We have access at all times to Being, because we are and we think Being. And at odd times we are given special access through the mode of sense perception. We are too close to ourselves and to our being, to think of Being as Being. If sense perceptions come in too fast, particularly strong and striking ones, the mind may not have the leisure to accept a wrenching out of time and space back to the inner life that had been put aside. So what should be a natural mode of access is shut. One mode of awareness of presence remains, one that is easy to overlook, the mode of art and artifice.

Sometimes when we see a painting for the first time, we feel as if we can walk into the world of the painter, whether abstract or representational. It is a kind of presence, something like the presence of someone we see whose personality overwhelms us, at least momentarily. We commonly refer to someone as having presence, as if presence were something put on like clothes, something separate from the whole person. But the fact that we are cowed by this presence is enough to remind us of one aspect of true presence—its totality. The painting is not a presence either, but it can have an effect of presence, giving an illusion of reality, namely, a world that we would like to be part of.

Something similar happens sometimes when we listen to music. It is a series of impressions of sound, as evanescent as can be, far more than the painting that will be around long after the instruments or the machine have stopped playing. And yet no more powerful impression of presence reaches most people than through music. Furthermore, we are comfortable with these impressions of presence in art. They demand little of us, and leave no scars, no questions. This is virtual presence, not real presence. No wonder that Proust, who believed that we cannot escape from ourselves, made one exception—through art. This is only partly true, of course, for since art is mirror and illusion, there is nothing permanent to respond to. One can only respond to what can return the favor. All art can offer is a reminder of immediacy of reality; it cannot offer reality. That is why art is ultimately unsatisfying; we are left to our own solitude, unless relieved by a real, not a virtual, presence.

There is a little story in Proust that makes this point. The narrator as a young man is staying at the Grand Hotel in Balbec. Around his room are bookcases with glass fronts which reflect "the ever-changing view of the sea"[30] outside. He needs not look out the windows to see the sea; all he needs is to look at the bookcases and feel he is surrounded, at least on three sides. What could be seen directly is refracted by the glass of the bookcases, so that the walls seemed to be lined with a "frieze of sea-scapes."[31] "What joy it was to me to see in all the glass fronts of the bookcases, as in the portholes of a ship's cabin, the open sea, unshadowed, and yet with half of its expanse in shadow."[32]

Seeing anything in reflection not only bypasses direct vision, it changes almost imperceptibly the shape, color, motion of the world thus refracted. It is as if we are being told that no vision can give a perfect image, its truest meaning, that everything is to some extent at a remove. In reflection as in art we get hints of reality, not reality. To some this is unsettling or, for those who do not appreciate art, exasperating. To others refraction, reality by indirection, may have just the opposite effect. Delay and indirection may heighten our sense of the satisfaction of presence just by making us wonder what we are missing. Who needs art if he or she can contemplate reality—or God—directly? But in a world where the contemplative life is feeble, refraction may keep open the ideal of a direct vision of real presence.

If art alone cannot keep the memory at least alive, a trip into the dark may. The same young man waking up in the same room in the middle of the night in a strange hotel "sees with glad relief a streak of daylight showing under the door. Thank God it is morning."[33] But it is only midnight. The steps in the hallway recede, and he is left to get control of his loneliness, to "lie all night in agony, with no one to bring him relief."[34] This is the dark night of the Proustian soul, alone in a hotel bedroom. Then to wake up in the morning to the refracted pictures of the seafront, like pictures at an exhibition, is to feel one has earned the right to make the natural journey back through the refractions to the actual reality of the sea itself. For worse than reality at a remove is the implacable anguish of being alone, and when that is relieved by recovering the reflected light of the bookcases, one may suppose the source of that light is waiting outside to be discovered.

Postscript

There are daylight truths and night truths. Hemingway said, "The night is not the same as the day: the things of the night cannot be explained in the day, because they do not then exist, and the night can be a dreadful time for lonely people once their loneliness has started."[35] There is anguish in the night and relief at daybreak. There is life closed down on one in the night, and the vision through glass in the morning. Beyond the glass, mirrors, and windows is actual being, if one is ready to look out. "Now we see through a glass darkly, but then face to face" (1 Cor. 13:13). Face to face is presence, the biblical language for it. Through a glass is through a mirror, and compared to the actual sun on the actual sea, the light on the waves through the glass is dark. But to one who has just come out of the travail of the lonely night, it is bright indeed and can restore the readiness of the soul to see face to face.

There is the face of art, itself a mirror of the artist's soul, inviting the viewer or listener to create another mirror through which to imagine reality on their own. There is the face of the past, hidden in the depths of memory, released by metaphoric memory, involuntarily, suddenly, unexpectedly, as by chance or by gift of grace, the grace of Being. This face is the map of the world of one individual, with that person's own precious history, seeking and failures, attempts to love, and deceptions and disappointments. It has its ways, a Méséglise Way and a Guermantes Way, seemingly irreconcilable, as the search for love differs from a search for worldly or social success. The face because it is no longer young is a map which another can read as a guide to what that person has held dear or has lost. Recollection like the bookcases of Balbec provides a simulacrum of presence, but not yet presence, a substitute for what we may be resigned to not being capable of experiencing directly. So much of the art and practice of Buddhism is directed to the liberation or recovery of that capacity.

We need not go East to meet presence. However elusive the subliminal orientation is, it is not beyond our power to awaken it. And when we do, all other experiences will seem trivial; the awakening of the desire for morning in the night of anguish, the reflected light of art and artifice, the occasional flashes of intuition in sense perception: There will be no loneliness in the presence of Being, for Being includes all the rest within it.

NOTES

1. Rahner, *Foundations of Christian Faith*, 33, 35, 42.
2. Rahner, *Foundations of Christian Faith*, 77.
3. Rahner, *Foundations of Christian Faith*, 21.
4. Lavelle, *La Présence Totale*, 25.
5. Rahner, *Foundations of Christian Faith*, 52, 35.
6. Rahner, *Foundations of Christian Faith*, 123.

7. Lavelle, *La Présence Totale*, 47.

8. Eckhart, *A Modern Translation*, 226.

9. Eckhart, *An Anthology of Sermons*, 181.

10. Eckhart, *An Anthology of Sermons*, 198.

11. Eckhart, *A Modern Translation*, 288.

12. Proust, I, 49.

13. Proust, I, 49.

14. Proust, I, 51.

15. Proust, III, 905.

16. Proust, III, 906.

17. Proust, III, 262.

18. Proust, III, 906.

19. Proust, I, 51.

20. Proust, I, 196.

21. Proust, I, 195.

22. Proust, III, 381.

23. Proust, I, 195.

24. Wordsworth, "Tintern Abbey."

25. Proust, III, 262.

26. Proust, III, 903.

27. Proust, III, 898.

28. Alain-Fournier, *Le Grand Meaulnes*, 110.

29. Lewis, *The Lion, the Witch, and the Wardrobe*.

30. Proust, I, 416.

31. Proust, I, 416.

32. Proust, I, 723.

33. Proust, I, 4.

34. Proust, I, 4.

35. Hemingway, *A Farewell to Arms*, 258.

2 | Being as Presence

Being as Presence

In 1927 a treatise called *Being and Time* was published in Germany. It began with a question that would haunt the author, Martin Heidegger, for the rest of his life: "Do we in our time have an answer to the question of what we really mean by the word 'being'? Not at all. So it is fitting that we should raise anew the question of the meaning of Being. Our provisional aim is the interpretation of time as the possible horizon for any understanding whatsoever of Being."[1] Then followed a long, dense, phenomenological analysis of the contents of the consciousness of everyday existence. After acknowledging that Being is the most universal of concepts and the darkest, Heidegger had nothing more to say about Being until the final sentence, "Does Time itself manifest itself as the horizon of Being?" Heidegger intended to answer this question in a second part. For thirty years students were told that the master had written Part Two but for unknown reasons was delaying its publication. In lectures and essays between 1927 and Heidegger's death, hints were dropped here and there of Heidegger's understanding of Being, but when he died it became clear that little more was forthcoming, that he had said all he could. One short essay, *On Time and Being*,[2] contained just about all there was to say.

For thirty years Heidegger's reputation rested on his detailed analysis of human beings' consciousness of their existence: their being-in-the-world, with things, with others, like themselves, their essential nature as Care (*Sorge*), their dread (*Angst*) of death, the call of their authentic self to work out their inmost possibilities and their resoluteness in facing them. This analysis became for many theologians and philosophers a program for the study of human existence. It was natural that they should think of Heidegger as an existentialist, like his contemporary Karl Jaspers, and in the tradition from Augustine, Pascal, and Kierkegaard to Nietzsche. Heidegger himself may have encouraged this by his references to them. His themes were their themes, the themes also of Jaspers and Karl Barth. But Heidegger resisted being associated with existentialism from the start. This seemed bewildering, even perverse, to many of his disciples, for had he not written more systematically than Jaspers, for example, about many of the same themes? But Heidegger continued to insist that he was not interested primarily in the nature of human existence but in the question of Being. He still intended to write a fundamental ontology, a new metaphysics that could replace those of Plato, Aristotle, Thomas Aquinas, Kant, and Hegel. But the new ontology never appeared.

Not only was his intention clear, so was his method. The foundation of his existential analysis—he had no objection to that phrase—was his assertion that understanding Being is a definite characteristic of mankind's being. "In his very being, Being is an issue for man."[3] And the analysis seemed to make clear that every phenomenon of consciousness had a temporal aspect. Therefore, was it not plausible to assume that since the meaning of Being is already and at all times somewhat available to us, it must be available through our hold on time? But as the years went by, it became slowly obvious that the method had gone nowhere, that Heidegger himself had realized this and was beginning all over. He had not lost interest in the question of Being, but he had given up any attempts to write a grandiose new fundamental ontology. More and more he seemed to be preoccupied with the question of how Being had come to be forgotten, how it had started out in pre-Socratic times as primordially close and had become for two thousand years the emptiest and most distant of words. There could be no argument about the record of the two thousand years, but it was by no means certain that Heidegger was on sure ground in supposing that there was once a time when Being meant something else. Had he retreated into wishful thinking as, at the same time, he began making cryptic, gnomic statements and falling back from philosophical discussion to interpretation of poets such as Hölderlin, Rilke, Trakl? The odd thing was that throughout all this his disciples increased in numbers. He had become holy in his time, except, of course, for those who despised him for his refusal to condemn the) Nazi horrors.

If all we knew of Heidegger came from the fragmented discussions of the post-war years—usually called the "Late Heidegger"—we would still have to go to him to learn what his predecessors in the long history of Western philosophy had not taught us, at least as unambiguously. If the assertion of the early Heidegger was "Man is Care," the grand assertion of the late Heidegger was "Being is Presence."

In the post-war lectures and seminars, Heidegger devoted much time to the story of how Being has been forgotten, for him the central story of the West. At least, that was his intention. But that, too, it seems to me, came to little. For it finally became clear that Heidegger realized that the problem of Being was not how to know Being but how to experience Being. That is why he instinctively fell back on interpretations of poetry and the fragments of the early Greek philosophers.

He would have been on safer ground had he spent as much time interpreting some of the medieval mystics, particularly Meister Eckhart who, he acknowledged, "thought rightly." I can only guess why he did not. Heidegger was born and educated a Catholic, intended to become a priest, and had studied theology. In fact, he continued to read Eckhart and Thomas Aquinas all his life. I think he may have looked in vain in the mystics for rigorous analysis and mistrusted the same analysis when he found it in Scotus and Aquinas. Unlike his contemporaries Gilson and Maritain, he seems not to have seen the existential piety behind or within the medieval philosophers. One was a mystic or one was a philosopher. He missed what both Gilson and Maritain saw and always insisted on—the scholastic, especially the Thomistic, emphasis on the intuition of Being. Heidegger may have missed the piety of Aquinas because he himself either had never had any or had lost it. How else can we explain his taking Hölderlin and Rilke seriously enough to interpret them, and not Eckhart or Aquinas? Heidegger had to discover the holy from the back door.

He seems finally to have understood that the human relationship to Being should change from thinking of Being as universal, empty, dark, in other words, from forgetting, to the primary response of wonder, astonishment, and awe. Again and again, he used words that indicate a revolution in his own approach to Being. Man is the shepherd of Being; we are meant to guard and care for Being. Thinking means thanking. To think Being is to feel grateful to Being. We are meant to sacrifice ourselves to Being, pressing the truth of Being out of all we experience, out of "the heart of unconcealment."[4]

Heidegger had long made a point of translating the Greek word for truth, *aletheia*, as "the unforgotten." Now he would go beyond this and insist on human responsibility for disclosing the fullness of being. In the exercise of that responsibility would be much joy.

What a far cry from fundamental ontology. This is not philosophy any more, it is meditation. Perhaps the Ignatian exercises of Heidegger's Jesuit upbringing had finally come to the surface. Even his earlier phenomenological analysis of human existence—and also the later interpretations of poetry—might now be read as an Ignatian "composition of place."[5] To those who were used to philosophical analysis, his last seminars might still seem the stuff of philosophy, but to those familiar with the methods of religious meditation, particularly Jesuit, the same seminars might seem to be the exercises of a retreat director.

It is not surprising either that he was asked over and over whether he was not really thinking of God, not just Being. And just as he had become impatient earlier when his *Being and Time* was called existentialist, so now he had to fend off, sometimes slyly, the suspicion that everything he said about Being could be said about God. When he wrote or spoke of Nothing, he used the Eckhartian image: Nothing is the *veil* of Being. So one began to suspect that he would really have liked to have called Being the veil of God, were it not that well-read disciples, especially the Catholic religious among them, would pounce on him and say, "So that is where you are heading!" They would have been right. He asked for a Catholic burial.

He wrote of Being as someone else might write of God. Being *calls*. Being *approaches*. Being *appears*. Being *gives*. The "soundless voice of Being" calls, and we must listen. No longer did fundamental ontology interest Heidegger, only fundamental thinking. Thinking means listening and then rejoicing at what one hears. Thinking means thanking Being and rejoicing in what is appearing.

This is ontological meditation, and its theme is Being as presence. This was Heidegger's formula for his discovery. Being is a *standing* presence; it *lingers* and it *lasts*. In meditation the truth of Being appears as an opening in a forest grove lets the light in. Being is like a *homestead, present*, abiding in that clearing. We approach Being with a feeling of uncanniness; the longer we mull over Being, the more mysterious Being seems, until we finally understand that the purpose of our life is to guard the mystery. Philosophy, as Heidegger finally understood it, must begin with this meditative intimacy without which all analysis will only lead once more to the forgetting of Being.

The outcome of ontological meditation is the revelation of Being as presence. Being presents itself to us making all things present. Heidegger was consistent in always supposing that the very inner constitution of the human mind involves our close understanding of Being, our existence, and the existence of everything else. All Being presents itself to us at all times, and most immediately in the present. All Being is a gift of itself to us, and it is our vocation to accept it gratefully and to guard its mystery. In the silence of its coming—its *parousia*—we meditate on all this joyfully: "at the still point of the turning world,"[6] where "words strain, crack, and sometimes break, under the burden, under the tension" (Eliot).[7] Presence is "the point of intersection of the timeless with time"[8] and is "an occupation for the saint."[9] It is also, like every occupation of a saint, the occupation for everyone.

Reality Has Deceived Me

In the story of presence, the two usual sources are religion and interpersonal relationship. Heidegger had nothing to say about either. That is why it is so surprising that in a treatise on metaphysics there appears an almost throw-away line that connects Being, presence, and love. "The joy we feel in the presence of the being—not merely the person—of someone we love."[10] There is a hint of humanness here that we do not associate with Heidegger. And it makes one wonder why he had been so silent throughout his career about this most powerful of the sources of presence. Had he forgotten love, as the West had forgotten Being? And why should he suddenly remember what it is like to be in the presence of someone one loves, and then to fall silent again? Had he been frustrated, disappointed; had he been deceived? Was he like Proust, who said he believed that shared loves exist for others, but not for himself? Or was he, like Proust at other times, someone who believed that reality always disappoints and deceives? He could believe in Being as present, but not in the presence of himself to someone else? The contrast is worth looking into.

Proust usually insisted that presence is impossible, and he had no ontological escape hatch as Heidegger had. Proust shared Kierkegaard's self-isolation, as Sartre later was to share his. The Proustian story is the story of a search, explicitly for lost time, but actually for a lost presence. The story begins with instances of anguish, and it ends with a trembling on the pinnacle of old age and death. It is a deeply pessimistic story, although radiated with moments of exhilaration and joy. The pessimism comes from the conviction that both love and reality will be withheld no matter how much one longs for love or wants to appreciate the present in its fullness. But the pessimism is balanced by longing and relieved in the end by a substitute for both love and reality withheld, namely, a sense of the past as if present. Lacking real presence, moral or noetic, remembered present offers a simulacrum as substitute.

The Proustian fictional adventure can, therefore, never erase the impression that is supported by life itself. "Reality has disappointed me."[11] What the French actually says is "Reality has deceived me." To be disappointed is to have expectation frustrated. To be deceived is to have a promise broken. The first is a statement about time, the second about morals. And the hurt of the second is deeper. One can be disappointed with anguish; one cannot be deceived without feeling personally affronted. Grand quests like

Proust's should not grow out of disappointments, but they may arise out of deception if the solution seems to offer some kind of reversal. To be deceived is to feel cut off from life. In Proust's case it is also an aspect, I believe, of his lifelong narcissism.

The statement "Reality has deceived me" was a reference not to broken promises but to a failure of the imagination. "Reality had deceived me because at the instant when my senses perceived it, my imagination which was the only organ that I possessed for the enjoyment of beauty could not apply itself to it, in virtue of that ineluctable law which ordains that we can only imagine what is absent."[12] Proust sets this up in contrast to the function of involuntary memory, which is to "savor," having "added to the dreams of the imagination the concept or idea of existence which they usually lack."[13] I am uncomfortable with his use of the word "*idée.*" Perhaps what he should have said is sense (*sens*), not idea or concept. This is what he thinks neither perception nor dream has. And he claims that involuntary memory provides the missing ingredient, the feeling of totality that surprised him so much in his experience of involuntary memory. He said that "reality takes shape in the memory alone,"[14] because "in all perception there exists a barrier of contingencies as a result of which there is never absolute contact between reality and our intelligence."[15] Does he mean that the mind is a victim of innumerable kinds and causes of separation between it and what is not it? And does one have control over these? All we do have is a dream of immediacy, beauty, intimacy, but as if across some barrier or void, longed for but unachievable. Proust goes on to mention "our inherent powerlessness to realize ourselves in natural enjoyment or in effective action."[16] "Reality must reside elsewhere than in action."[17]

This is a very dark view of life. It is much darker than Heidegger's pessimism about the forgetting of Being. At least Heidegger assumed from the beginning of his career the human capacity for thinking Being, and before he had finished, he affirmed the human guardianship of Being as a presence. Proust, on the other hand, seems to have been convinced that only in what is totally within the enclosure of the self can there be a sense of reality or of the beauty of that reality. "Man is alone,"[18] a prisoner of consciousness, for whom reprieve can come only from within the prison walls. It is not surprising that Proust should have concluded that "Man is the creature who cannot escape from himself, who knows other people only in himself, and when he asserts the contrary he is lying."[19]

If one follows the logic of Proust's theories about the self, it is easy to see how the barriers between self and others can be thought to be a consequence of barriers between mind and reality. If Proust is right, then we must accept the drastic consequences of intellectual self-isolation. We know that some people are more narcissistic than others, and some have been rejected from childhood more than their fellows. Out of personal bias, dark theories are born and then affirmed as universal. When I think of Heidegger's comparatively bright view of presence, it is all the easier to remark on the characteristic narcissism of Proust and suspect that he had raised self-isolation—unlike Kierkegaard who knew he was an exception—into a universal principle.

By asserting that "between us and other people there exists a barrier of contingencies," Proust could make himself believe that "the bonds between ourselves and another person exist only in our minds."[20] "I know that shared loves exist"—presence—"but, alas, I do not know their secret."[21] In his novels he went further: "There are people for whom there is not such a thing as shared love. We can only enjoy that simulacrum of happiness . . . as if loved . . . [and] pretend that it formed part of a vast and enduring happiness of which this fragment only was visible to me."[22] "It is the tragedy of other people that they are showcases for the very perishable collections of one's own mind."[23] Then he piles it on. "Love is a doll fashioned in our brain,"[24] fashioned out of "a terrible need for another person."[25] So "we live only with what we do not love, in order to kill the intolerable love."[26] "One seeks to see the beloved, but one ought not to seek—forgetfulness alone brings about the ultimate extinction of desire."[27]

Worse follows: The person who once loved no longer exists. "We believe we can change things around us, but gradually our desires change."[28] Even the self which, theoretically, is permanent, is mainly composed of successive selves. Not only is "nobody exempt from change, our total soul has only a more or less fictitious value."[29] We are unfaithful to what we once were.[30]

The last hundred pages of the long novel are a demonstration of the changes effected by time. Not only does society look like a masquerade of puppets wearing masks which distort their real faces, their former faces, it seems as if society had been playing a game of musical chairs. No one but God and the narrator knows the true position of anyone in society. "Time has, it seems, special express trains,"[31] which no longer stop at the expected stations but rush on to death. "The only true paradises are the paradises that are lost."[32]

Proust had used this formula before; it expressed something central to his attitude toward life. "Experience had taught me the impossibility of attaining in the real world to what lay deep within myself."[33] No wonder that he believed that beauty, like charm, comes not from the senses, although it enters through the senses. Had he once been able to apprehend with some immediacy? How else could he describe reality so well that we can believe in it? Perhaps by the time that he was ready to write his novel he had lost the capacity for presence, and could honestly conclude that "the truths which the intellect apprehends directly have something less profound than those which life communicates to us against our will in an impression which is material because it enters through the senses but yet has a spiritual meaning which it is possible for us to extract."[34]

Out of context one might suppose that this material impression could refer to a sense of presence. But the context makes plain that he is thinking of the metaphoric activity of involuntary memory. A sense impression in the present brings a memory of a similar experience from the forgotten past. To use Heidegger's language, he remembers Being, but with the crucial addition of feeling it as if it were present again. The "essential character" of such moments "was that I was not free to choose them. This must be the mark of their authenticity."[35]

This is Proustian grace. But grace, Proustian or Christian, adds something that the self would otherwise not experience and that is more important than the time of its coming. In Proust's mind, chance (not grace) added a reality or a truth (he is not particular about which) that is "real without being actual, ideal without being abstract."[36] Once again he plays with terms that to someone else would be theological. So much that is ultimate for Proust is a simulacrum of religion. He had not been brought up a Catholic for nothing.

He parts decisively from that perspective when he speaks of "the timeless man (*l'homme éternel*) within me."[37] For all his assurance that "my anxiety on the subject of my death had ceased at the moment when I had unconsciously recognized the taste of the little madeleine,"[38] death did not go away, just his anxiety over death and his discouragement over his writing. He felt his being to be "extratemporal,"[39] but feeling so did not make him extratemporal. He too died and was buried a Catholic. He was no more eternal than any other author. I do not think he even thought of that when he claimed that "through art alone are we able to escape from ourselves."[40]

The Proustian world has elements of grace, the light from the past, but it is full of darknesses, not only his dogmatic pessimism, but a landscape of frustration of desire, acquisitiveness, manipulation, sadism, jealousy, lying, mutual torment, social climbing and snobbism, sexual instability and inversion, illness, loss of persons, loss of the self: the whole spectrum of anguish. How dark Proust's universe is we realize when in eulogizing the death of Bergotte he speaks of "these obligations which have no sanction in our present life, and seem to belong to a different world, a world based on kindness, scrupulousness, self-sacrifice, a world entirely different from our own and which we leave in order to be born on this earth."[41] These are rumors of another kind of world, a world of presence.

He (or his narrator) is bemused by the changes in himself as in others. "I did not realize how much I had changed. My friend declared that I had not changed, and I realized that in his own eyes he had not changed."[42] He had never found his own way into a world of self-sacrifice. He seems to have forgotten that he once knew presence himself. And except for one curious passage near the end, the narrator's meeting when he is elderly with the young Mlle. de Saint-Loup, he never breathes a hope that the future may be different. He is totally absorbed in what has been and what cannot be.

Invasions of Being

A Whole Secret System of Life

Some people are more susceptible to presence than others. Their sensibilities depend to a large extent on the discriminatory power of their five senses. The one sense that in most of us is dominant, sight, is the only one that does not involve any sort of invasion of our being. No wonder that we can separate the acknowledgment of Being from its presence to us. Of the other four senses, taste and touch involve more palpable sensations that are more transitory than smell and sound. These insidiously invade us, bathing us in signals from Being. In that most isolated of men, Kafka, there are few traces of smell or sound, no scents, no music.

If one is sensitive to smells and to sounds, one cannot avoid their messages. Only those who cannot smell or who have no ear for music have to admit that they cannot share with others signals that invade us only to set us free to imagine worlds without us. This is the peculiar property of these two senses. We identify a room by its smell, as a dog identifies each of us by our own smells. Of course, each of us, not just our rooms, has a distinctive smell but only dogs recognize us by them. Through all the changes in the bodies of a man and woman, the voice alone usually survives unchanged. But beyond these means of identification is the strange power that smell and sound have to set the mind winging away from itself. Proust knew, and did not know, this. Through smell and sound we can escape ourselves.

When threatened with loss of sight, we feel the bonds between us and reality dissolving, forgetting that we still have four other senses even if we have not learned to use them. Of all our senses, our sense of smell is probably the least developed. It is our goal to live in such a sterile environment that we can proudly boast, "I don't smell anything." I would call this a neo-Platonic world, quite different from the one Bernanos lamented when he said, as I read long ago, "When I am dead, tell the kingdom of earth that I have loved it more than I ever dared to say." Unlike Plotinus, he could not have been ashamed of his body. When Proust thought of his childhood (in Combray-Illiers), he remembered his aunt's house "with countless odours emanating from the virtues, wisdom, habits"[43] containing "a whole secret system of life, invisible, super-abundant, and profoundly moral."[44] He does not let us forget, as he begins his leisurely tale about that childhood, what these smells were. "Smells natural enough indeed, and weather-tinted like those of the neighboring countryside, but already humanised, domesti-cated, snug, and exquisite, limpid jelly skillfully blended from all the fruits of the years which have left the orchard for the storeroom, smells changing with the season, but plenishing and homely, smells lazy and punctual as a village clock, roving and settled, heedless and provident, linen smells, morning smells, pious smells, rejoicing in a peace which brings only additional anxiety, and in a prosaicness which serves as a deep reservoir of poetry."[45]

How different from our vacuumed rooms, this "air of rooms saturated with the fine bouquet of a silence so nourishing, so succu-lent that I never went into them without a sort of greedy anticipa-tion."[46] We await a metaphysician with a good discriminating nose. How easy Proust makes it for us to imagine him as a child walking up and down in the room outside his aunt's bedroom "while the fire [was] baking like dough the appetizing smells with which the air of the room was thickly clotted and which the moist and sunny freshness of the morning had already 'raised' and started to set, puffed them and glazed them and fluted them and swelled them into an invisible though not impalpable country pie, an immense 'turnover' which, barely waiting to savour the crisper, more deli-cate, more reputable but also drier aromas of the cupboard, the chest of drawers and the patterned wallpaper, I always returned with an unconfessed gluttony to wallow in the central, glutinous, insipid, indigestible and fruity smell of the flowered bedspread."[47] Even ghosts are said sometimes to leave a smell of brimstone.

A World of Dreams

Smells invade our nostrils, cling to our clothes. Others can tell where we have been and with whom. Music, on the other hand, invades the ears only as far as the eardrums. It lingers only long enough to liberate the imagination which then bears us away even from ourselves. So it is not that the music lingers. The music goes and the dream evoked by the music lingers. The music has been only the impalpable vehicle of some presence. No one has spoken better about the effects of music than Proust.

Music is the language of time, of what we have lost and of "new vistas,"[48] "the possibility of a sort of rejuvenation."[49] And while the music lasts, we last too. In music we can live for a time, the present time, in a world where grief and anxiety disappear, where we live in tranquillity with ourselves.

Proustian fiction and Proustian metaphysics are inconceivable without the music of Vinteuil, the only sensory experience shared by both the narrator and Swann. Most Proustian sensory experiences are joyful. Not so the music of Vinteuil which is heavy with longing and premonition of loss, all the heavier because it is also capable of evoking images of hope.

When Swann first heard a piano arrangement of a violin sonata by Vinteuil, his love for Odette had not yet become an obsession. The "little phrase" from this sonata became "the national anthem of their love."[50] It seemed to suggest new vistas and the possibility of the rejuvenation of a jaded middle-aged man. He felt himself "in the presence of one of those invisible realities in which he had ceased to believe. . . . He felt as though he had met, in a friend's drawing-room, a woman whom he had seen and admired in the street and had despaired of ever seeing again."[51] Swann did not yet fear that he would not see Odette again; he did not even know he was in love with her. But he already knew through the music that he could feel like that.

When the man who tells the story, long after Swann's love affair had ended, heard the same music, he said, "I never possessed it in its entirety; it was like life itself"[52] which one gets to know bit by bit. And when he began to use it in his affair with Albertine, who played parts of it for him as Odette had for Swann, he found it to be "some definite spiritual reality . . . the very movement of our being."[53] "The little phrase had the power to liberate in him the room that was needed to contain it."[54]

Probably neither Odette nor Albertine knew what was going on, beyond that it was a symbol of their affairs. There is no evidence that either had the capacity to imagine "a sort of reality superior to concrete things,"[55] satisfying a "thirst for an unknown delight."[56]

Perhaps indeed Swann never loved Odette—certainly Marcel never loved Albertine—as much as he loved being in love. For love was for them both a dream of "entering into contact with a world for which we men were not made,"[57] where there might be "deep repose, a mysterious refreshment"[58] such as neither woman could imaginably provide. The language may be mystical, but the dalliance was manipulative, as each man devised strategies for relieving "much that was painful, much secret and unappeased sorrow that underlay the sweetness of the phrase."[59]

When Swann first heard the entire sonata, his love affair was in ashes, and the music gave him an "agonizingly painful"[60] sense of "lost happiness."[61] Even so he could speculate that musical motifs were "actual ideas of another world, another order."[62] In "that vast, unfathomed and forbidding night of our soul,"[63] where lost love and dreaming sensibility live side by side, he had not yet lost his capacity for understanding that human beings belong to "an order of supernatural beings whom we have never seen"[64] but whose "magic presence"[65] occasionally visits those who have a taste for music, which is "linked to the future, to the reality of the human soul."[66] It urges us to go forward at the same time that it reminds us of what we have to lose. "We shall perish, but we have as hostages these divine captives who will follow and share our fate. And death in their company is somehow less bitter, less inglorious, perhaps less probable."[67]

Swann discovered that music has a life of its own, its own presence. He had "regarded musical motifs as actual ideas, of another world, of another order, ideas veiled in shadow, unknown, impenetrable to the human mind, but none the less perfectly distinct from one another."[68] When his love for Odette faded, he had this confirmed. Then when he heard the Vinteuil sonata, instead of thinking about Odette, "Swann's thoughts were borne for the first time on a wave of pity and tenderness towards Vinteuil, towards that unknown exalted brother who must have suffered so greatly. What could his life have been? From the depths of what well of sorrow could he have drawn that god-like strength, that unlimited power of creation?"[69]

It is rare indeed for any of Proust's characters to escape from himself, to feel that he has "an essential self"[70] and is a "native of an unknown country"[71] which he shares with another human being. And yet Swann could feel himself in the presence of an invisible creature, "so different from anything that any woman had ever made me desire, perhaps the only Unknown Woman that it has been my good fortune to meet."[72] At that moment he could believe that the music of Vinteuil "was no longer an almost anxious appeal addressed to an empty sky, it was an ineffable joy which seemed to come from paradise."[73] The goal was in his heart.

Postscript

First, we have to speak of our separation from Being. There is the mode of forgetting that the philosopher must acknowledge. There is the mode of disappointment and deception that anyone can experience in his relations with other people. There is also the mode of disappointment and deception that comes from some theoretical insistence, some personal dogmatism, that we are incapable, perhaps that everyone is incapable, of presence. The range goes from Heidegger to Proust, and it exposes something of the underside of the modern mind, particularly its disinterest in the question of Being and its skepticism about presence.

Second, we have considered two different approaches to Being: the way of philosophical meditation and scents and music. Heidegger was saying something more unusual than has yet been fully realized when he suggested that Being is what we experience all the time. We would be far better off as philosophers if we asked how to experience Being instead of how to know Being. He at least suggested one way, meditation. But there are others which he did not talk about, and this is why it is useful to turn to Proust, and particularly to what he has to say about those two senses that invade our bodies and liberate our minds at the same time. Through Proust we learn something about Being as presence that Heidegger may not have known. Being not only lingers, it beckons us onward. The human experience with music that lures us beyond ourselves into dreams of our future or other worlds thus supplements the Heideggerian meditation which emphasizes our guardianship of the mystery of Being.

NOTES

1. Heidegger, *Being and Time*, 1.
2. Heidegger, *On Time and Being*.
3. Heidegger, *On Time and Being*, 32.
4. Heidegger, *On Time and Being*, 32.
5. Ignatius Loyola, *Spiritual Exercises*, 125, 170.
6. Eliot, "Burnt Norton."
7. Eliot, "Burnt Norton."
8. Eliot, "Dry Salvages."
9. Eliot, "Dry Salvages."
10. Heidegger, *Existence and Being*, 364.
11. Proust, III, 905.
12. Proust, III, 905.
13. Proust, III, 905.
14. Proust, I, 201.
15. Proust, III, 1023.
16. Proust, III, 1023.
17. Proust, III, 911.
18. Proust, III, 459.
19. Proust, III, 459.
20. Proust, III, 459.
21. Proust, *Selected Letters*, 337.
22. Proust, II, 864.
23. Proust, III, 568.
24. Proust, II, 384.
25. Proust, II, 759.
26. Proust, III, 93.
27. Proust, III, 458.
28. Proust, III, 460.
29. Proust, II, 783.
30. Proust, II, 888.
31. Proust, III, 986.
32. Proust, III, 903.
33. Proust, III, 910.
34. Proust, III, 912.
35. Proust, III, 913.
36. Proust, III, 906.
37. Proust, III, 957.
38. Proust, III, 904.
39. Proust, III, 904.
40. Proust, III, 932.
41. Proust, III, 186.
42. Proust, III, 985.
43. Proust, I, 53.

44. Proust, I, 53.
45. Proust, I, 53.
46. Proust, I, 53.
47. Proust, I, 54.
48. Proust, I, 229.
49. Proust, I, 229.
50. Proust, I, 238.
51. Proust, I, 229–31.
52. Proust, I, 571.
53. Proust, III, 381.
54. Proust, I, 258.
55. Proust, I, 258.
56. Proust, I, 258.
57. Proust, I, 259.
58. Proust, I, 259.
59. Proust, I, 259.
60. Proust, I, 375.
61. Proust, I, 376.
62. Proust, I, 379.
63. Proust, I, 380.
64. Proust, I, 381.
65. Proust, I, 380.
66. Proust, I, 381.
67. Proust, I, 381.
68. Proust, I, 379.
69. Proust, I, 379.
70. Proust, III, 258.
71. Proust, III, 258.
72. Proust, III, 262.
73. Proust, III, 362.

ontology – 1. a branch of metaphysics
concerned w. the nature + relation
of being. 2. a particular theory
about the nature of being
or the kinds of existents

ontological argument – an argument for the
existence of God based upon the
meaning of the term God

ont- or onto- combined form from Greek : ont- on,
prep. of einai – to be. 1.) being : existence
(ontology); 2; organism (ontogeny)

3 | *Presence and Mystery*

Presence and Mystery

Twenty years before Heidegger affirmed that Being is presence, Gabriel Marcel had spoken of the necessity of restoring to human experience its ontological weight. As Heidegger meditated on Being and presence, Marcel meditated on presence and mystery. I doubt whether either was influenced by the other. Indeed Marcel's idea of presence is more complex than Heidegger's, or should I say more developed? Marcel, unlike Heidegger, was interested in the relations between persons as much as he was interested in ontology. His notion of presence was clearly influenced by Buber's *I and Thou*, published in 1923, eight years before Marcel's first journal entries on the ontological mystery. Marcel stands between Buber and Heidegger in more than time. His notion of presence involved a concept of Being and a dynamic of human relations. Buber who had anticipated the latter saw the ontological dimension of I and Thou, but he did not emphasize it as did Marcel. It is not surprising that Marcel felt he needed to express his two concerns in different kinds of writing, the ontological in his "metaphysical journal" and the interpersonal in his plays.

In a way he brought them together in his understanding of the "ontological need"[1] in human experience. On the one hand, there is the metaphysical uneasiness that can rise to a crescendo as a hunger for Being (as in Unamuno); on the other hand, there is in human relations at their best an acknowledgment of the mystery of

Being, in the sense of the inexhaustibility of each person. Marcel
was a man of prayer, as I myself saw one day when he visited me in
my parish church, but I do not think he was a contemplative. He
has written, autobiographically, of the deep impression nature and
music made on him as he grew up. But when he writes of the mystery of Being, he moves rather quickly from the general to the
nature of relations between persons. Marcel had no interest in con-
structing a fundamental ontology. He was preoccupied, as Heidegger was not, with the contrast between those who are encumbered
with themselves and those who are capable of charity and fidelity.
He knew how different his existentialism was from Sartre's or from
Heidegger's. When he thought of "the weight of Being,"[2] he
thought of Being as something that resists a reductive analysis. Of
course, Heidegger would have agreed. And he would have agreed
with Heidegger that it is the human vocation to guard the mystery
of Being, except for one thing: I believe he would have been impatient with Heidegger's refusal to come down to earth and talk
about the beings we are close to, responsible for—other human
beings. In their mystery there is much to meditate on and guard.
While for Heidegger man is the shepherd of Being, for Marcel,
much more are we our sister and brother's keeper. Marcel might
have said that Heidegger, like Cain, had felt the presence of
Yahweh. Even so, Marcel knew that the mysterious and the ontological are identical. For most people the access to Being is through
other people. What I have called an original experience of Being is
too subliminal for most minds to be sure of.

The mystery of Being, the ontological mystery, is not always
accessible through the mystery of another person either. However
positive, in theory, the mystery is, there are many who would not
understand what we are talking about. Here is where Marcel and
Buber may help. Just as Buber distinguished between the two relations, "I and It" and "I and Thou," so Marcel distinguished
between our relations to persons as objects and as presences. In the
world of "It" there is not much difference between our interest in
and manipulation of people and things. In the world of "Thou"
(the second person singular "you") the difference can be tremen-
dous. Buber stated the difference early in *I and Thou*, when he said:
"The primary word I-Thou can only be spoken with the whole

being. . . . He who gives himself to it may withhold nothing of himself."[3] The emphasis is on *the whole being*, mine and yours. Each must speak to the other and listen to the other with full attention, no corners reserved or hidden. We know this is possible, however difficult and even explosive. We know also that there is no need to do this in most of our dealings with people, and certainly not with things. We would be using up too much of our spirit if we did, and would not only become exposed unnecessarily but would be rebuffed as a stone is rebuffed against an iron shield.

Marcel developed a very simple distinction between "problem" and "mystery" to call attention to this. "A problem is something which I meet, which I find complete before me, but which I can therefore lay siege to and reduce. A mystery is something in which I myself am involved."[4] You can solve a problem; all you can do initially with a mystery is acknowledge it, as something in which you are or could be caught up. When people talk of the problem of evil, even when they are theologians, they are usually on the way to degrading a mystery. Anyone who tries to understand malevolence, for example, the Nazi hatred of Jews, should stop trying to find reasons for the dehumanization and the sadism. The mystery of malevolence is in quite a different world from the problem of anger, let's say, or even resentment. There is even a line between malevolence and vengeance, to say nothing of a line between malevolence and charity. In the real world the line is between thinking of people as things to be disposed of and thinking of them as presences. Perhaps the trouble begins when some people who are not prepared to acknowledge mystery encounter it in someone so different from themselves—the Jews in Nazis, blacks in some whites—that they feel they can handle mystery only by denying it and turning it into one more problem to be solved, and because it involves persons not things, a final solution.

We have problems with the word "mystery" too. For many, a mystery is simply the unknowable. And when it turns out to be knowable after all, as a mystery book, a detective story, a thriller, we go on calling it a mystery in our relief that after all there is nothing really unknowable. The deepest mysteries in fiction involve either some sense of a supernatural that we fear cannot be explained or evil men and women who would treat others as objects. I have always found the espionage thrillers in which there is Nazi malevolence more frightening than thrillers of the Cold War period. But this may be a matter of personal taste and history.

There are evil presences as well as good; no presence can be defined or foreseen. It is not more possible to comprehend an evil person than a loving person. Both are beyond merit. We do not deserve to be loved or hated by either one. Both extremes, of hate and love, are apparently inexhaustible and incomprehensible. These are conclusions we make after confronting them. What is not a conclusion is the effect presence has on us. We are either destroyed or renewed.

A presence cannot be created by us, not conjured up, not manipulated. There is an autonomy about the human person as a presence, as a mystery, that can only be invoked or evoked. We know it immediately as someone different, because it makes itself felt; it does not wait for us to guess. "Presence is something which reveals itself immediately in a look, a smile, an intonation, or a handshake."[5] This real presence is "a kind of influx."[6] Someone not really present, even if that person is before us talking away, does not make his or her whole being felt. But "when somebody's presence does really make itself felt, it can refresh my inner being, it reveals me to myself, it makes me more fully myself than I should be if I were not exposed to its impact."[7] The other can renew me. We remember persons who have had just such influence on us at times. We do not feel the same when they are near. Sometimes we are fooled. Marcel has things to say about the effect of charm, one of the signs of presence. But charm cannot always be trusted; it is too often not a sign of anyone else's whole attention to us or a promise of good. More often we are so encumbered with our fragmented and shaky souls, that we may be closed to presence when it is offered, and totally unable to give our whole attention, the gift of ourselves as a whole, to anyone else. Presence needs practice, and practice needs a wider experience of the mystery of Being than is available to many of us in the late twentieth century. Just to try to be faithful to anyone else requires what Marcel calls "a perpetuation of presence,"[8] beyond the exigencies of our distracted lives. To practice presence with anyone else, one must be aware of one's own mystery. "Presence and mystery are equivalent." Presence cannot be possessed. What is called self-possession is not the same as self-presence; it is as different as self-assurance from humility. A concept of God that does not think of God as absolute presence allows us to suppose God is something we can own—"my God" and "your God." To restore the ontological weight to God would mean restoring, as Karl Barth tried to do, transcendence to the world. To restore a conviction of human diginity to the world, we would do well to think of each person as a place of mystery, inexhaustible and open.

Perhaps Marcel's single most important insight, more important than his distinction between problem and mystery, or his sense of being as presence and presence as mystery, is his insistence that what truly makes a person human is his or her capacity for being open to others. His word for this openness is *disponibilité*.[9] The English "availability" sounds so cold. I recall Heidegger's conclusion that perhaps "Being and Time" should yield to "Time and Openness." I recall also Buber's line about "the real, filled present, [which] exists only in so far as actual presentness, meeting and relation, exists. The present arises only in virtue of the fact that the Thou becomes present."[10] And when he goes on to say that "true beings are lived in the present, the life of objects is in the past,"[11] he means us to remember that it is only in an I-Thou relationship that the true present can be lived. This is part of what Marcel means by *disponibilité*. "The person who is at my disposal is the one who is capable of being with me with the whole of himself."[12] He says, "There is a way of listening which is a way of giving."[13] We know this is true. There is a way of speaking too that is a way of giving. And when we give or receive, we cease to be strangers. Someone may "understand what I am saying, but he does not understand *me*."[14] For the giving and the receiving reveal the self behind them, "the total spiritual availability."[15] We need not use hyperbole as Marcel does—"absolute disposability,"[16] pure charity—to acknowledge the difference between communication and communion. Even a modest gift of oneself, tentatively, shyly offered, can be qualitatively different from listening with half the soul, withholding some parts or recesses from exposure to the light of day. Some people never give themselves completely, sometimes because they fear there will be nothing left if they do. From Marcel's perspective, a full experience of presence requires reciprocity, "the exchange which is the mark of all spiritual life."[17] Grace that ends with the giving is failed grace. Grace—the grace of loving attention—fails if it looks for some advantage and not a similarly free response. The paradox of the mystery of presence is that while it cannot be comprehended, in that sense cannot be handled, it can be the source of life and in that sense touched. I would say that we might consider that we are given a subliminal knowledge of Being not so that we may spend the rest of our lives meditating on Being, but so that we may be grounded in an experience of presence that will sustain us in our relations with other human beings with whom we spend most of our lives and with whom we can journey more openly, not just subliminally, into the heart of Being.

No one has written as eloquently or paradoxically about "exchange" as Charles Williams. His "doctrine of substituted love"[18] requires each of us to carry the burdens of others. W. H. Auden summed it up as "Nobody can carry his own burden; he only can, and therefore must, carry someone else's."[19] "To take over the grief or the fear or the anxiety of another"[20] is an act of substitution. "All life is to be vicarious."[21] This may fly in the face of our very modern insistence—and pride—that we should do everything ourselves. To try to do everything ourselves, however, is to fly in the face of the laws of the universe, and it results in what Kierkegaard called "sickness unto death." Marcel and Williams were convinced that only exchange or substitution can be a realistic antidote to despair. But first, "you must be content to be helped,"[22] and that is sometimes harder than to carry someone else's fear. And yet it can be done. "It's a fact of experience. If you give a weight to me, you can't be carrying it yourself."[23]

The doctrine of substitution goes beyond sympathetic listening. It can remove from someone the devastating loneliness and fear of suffering, and by so doing open the soul to the peace of Being. We know that the more depressed and self-isolated we are, the more self-centered we become, and the less able to feel anything but anger and pain. To refuse at that point to give up one's burden can destroy whatever is left of the soul. "Another will be in me who will suffer for me, as I shall suffer for him," said Clement.[24] Substitution is a test of the sincerity of presence.

Presence:
In Te, Domine, Speravi

Marcel, philosopher that he was, rarely used examples of *disponibilité* from ordinary life. He might have mentioned the attentions, the ministrations, the loving care of parents with children, nurses with patients, pastors with parishioners. We might then connect more readily with his notion of availability, and we would more readily see the human warmth behind the gift of whole to whole. Perhaps he was right in trying to avoid anything that could seem sentimental. When I think of the one part of the lives of Western man that undeniably speaks of presence, the religious world, I realize that there too it is easy to confuse presence with sentimentality. Evangelical hymns of the mid-nineteenth century such as "What a friend we have in Jesus!" or "He leadeth me! O blessed thought!" or "O for a closer walk with God!" however easily they dissolve distracted minds to tears at funerals do nothing to encourage sacrifice. Their sentimentality is more likely to satisfy the baser desire of self-importance: *me, me, me.* There is no sense of transcendence, no mystery, nothing essentially strengthening. How different they are from the great hymns of presence in the Psalter.

The psalms have formed the prayer of Israel and the Church for over two thousand years. There is an objectivity, a toughness about their vision of God that does not appeal to forced sentiment, but can give assurance for the journey of life. No one brought up with these as part of his or her daily or weekly piety, Jewish, Catholic, Orthodox, Anglican, Puritan, can ever develop a taste for the intrusive sentimentality of hymns such as the ones I have mentioned. One does not take liberties with the God of the psalms, who is not on our level at all. But he is God, and God is our refuge; "our hope and strength, a very present help in trouble. Therefore will we not fear even though the earth be moved, and though the hills be carried into the midst of the sea?" (Ps. 46:1–2).

And to this unseen, unknown God human beings appeal again and again, "Hide thy face from me. . . . Cast me not away from thy presence" (Ps. 51:9, 11) because "In Thee, O Lord, do I put my trust" (Ps. 31:1). In the early hours of the morning in monasteries and convents, the religious have sung these psalms and still do:

"Let us come before his presence with thanksgiving, and show ourselves glad in him with psalms" (Ps. 95:2). Those of us who have
presided over rites for the dead recall the unexpected power of feeling from the friends and relatives as they say, "The Lord is my
shepherd, therefore can I lack nothing. He shall feed me in a green
pasture, and lead me forth beside the waters of comfort" (Ps.
23:1–2). Or *Levavi oculos*: "I will lift up mine eyes unto the hills;
from whence cometh my help? My help cometh even from the
Lord, who hath made heaven and earth" (Ps. 121:1–2). This is the
point. It is the Absolute presence who has made heaven and earth
or, dare we say it with Buber, the Eternal Thou, who alone can
make us believe there is any safety in our troubles. Only this kind of
cosmic assurance will work, the kind we get from Psalm 139: "If I
climb up into heaven, thou art there; if I go down to hell, thou art
there also, if I take the wings of the morning, and remain in the
uttermost parts of the sea, even there also shall thy hand lead me,
and thy right hand shall hold me." The psalms almost have the
power to convert the soul to God. For when we say them with others, it is not difficult to believe that, "Thou shalt not be afraid for
any terror by night, nor for the arrow that flieth by day, for the pes-
tilence that walketh in darkness, nor for the sickness that destroyeth
in the noon-day. . . . For thou, Lord, art my hope; thou hast set
thine house of defense very high" (Ps. 91:5–6, 9).

I believe that however credible the psalms are in the privacy of
one's chamber, they derive their power from our awareness that
much of humankind has said and sung these together as one voice.
The person whose spiritual life begins in heaviness—"Why art thou
so full of heaviness, O my soul, and why art thou so disquieted
within me?" (Ps. 42:5)—may be able to finish the course, as Jesus
did, by saying, "Into thy hands I commend my spirit; for thou hast
redeemed me, O Lord, thou God of truth" (Ps. 31:5), having
become persuaded in the meantime that "The Lord shall preserve
thy going out, and thy coming in, from this time forth for ever-
more" (Ps. 121:8). If you have to know what presence is, read the
psalms; they are about the availability of God. And if you cannot
believe in God, at least let the shape of God's presence be a model
for presence with others. The ontological need is the same. Is this
not the shape of Richard Rolle's "In the love of God is the love of
my neighbor?"[25]

Mystery

Theophanies

Behind the psalms are the appearances of Yahweh, the intrusions of transcendence. And, to speak truly, they are very remote from the modern mind. Curious that this is so and that nevertheless the psalms can still touch chords. But the modern mind believes only in facts and can accept Mount Sinai but not God on Mount Sinai, mountains and clouds but not God speaking from inside the clouds. It seems easier to accept the world as un-created, as just always there, than to imagine a creator. No longer is anyone moved by the cosmological argument for the existence of God: if something is, something else must have made it. We say, "It is here, and that is all we need to know." The rest is speculation. I am not ignorant of the persistence of scientific speculation, but that is very far from an acceptance by ordinary people, like myself, of a creator God.

When we read Exodus, however, we do get some feeling for what such a God meant to Moses. Moses had been leading a restless people to a promised land—which he himself would never enter—and in the crisis of their fatigue and confusion he was summoned by Yahweh to come for instruction on Mount Sinai. There was thunder on the mountain, lightning, cloud, trumpet, smoke. And out of the cloud Yahweh spoke unambiguously (Exod. 19). This encounter became the model for the later theophanies of some of the prophets. Isaiah said of this, "At your Presence the mountains would melt, and make the nations tremble at your presence" (Isa. 64:1). And Jeremiah: "And will you not tremble at my presence?" (Jer. 5:22). And Ezekiel: "I saw visions from God: wind, fire, a storm, a throne, a being that looked like a man, [and] something like the glory of Yahweh" (Ezek. 1:26). Likewise Daniel: "Streams of fire poured out from his presence. I saw coming on the clouds, one like a son of man" (Dan. 7:10), with "a voice like a trumpet" (Rev. 4:1).

But in 1 Kings, the theophany is different. Elijah too was told to go out onto the mountain. He too saw wind, earthquake, and fire. But "Yahweh was not in the wind, not in the earthquake, not in the fire. After the fire came a gentle breeze" (1 Kings 19:12) (or, in an older translation, "a still small voice"). But Moses too had heard this voice, as a God of tenderness and compassion, slow to anger, rich in kindness and faithfulness. Both Moses and Elijah were given to understand that Yahweh is the God of Israel, not just the creator of the world, a mystery that cares and holds all in its embrace. To say this metaphysically: the mystery of Being embraces all within it, embraces and protects.

Ordinary Mysteries and Obscure Pleasures

To live in an age when there are no theophanies is not the same as to live without mystery. There are ordinary mysteries in everyday life. No one knew this better than Proust. He did not believe in presence, and yet he believed in mystery which is the basic stuff of presence. This I take to be the significance of two episodes which he relates and refers to again and again in his novel: the steeples of Martinville and a line of trees near Balbec.

Sometimes we see something or something happens to us that is far from extraordinary yet presents an insoluble puzzle and at the same time gives us pleasure, a pleasure that is out of proportion to the ordinariness of what we have seen.

Take the ride to Martinville first. One afternoon the narrator as a young man was out walking with his father. The local doctor picked them up and took them with him to Martinville, where he was to visit a patient before returning home. "At a bend in the road I experienced, suddenly, that special pleasure which was unlike any other, on catching sight of the twin steeples of Martinville, bathed in the setting sun and constantly changing their position with the movement of the carriage and the windings of the road, and then of a third steeple, that of Vieuxvicq, which, although separated from them by a hill and a valley, and rising from rather high ground in the distance, appeared none the less to be standing by their side. . . . I felt that I was not penetrating to the core of my impression, that something more lay behind that mobility, that luminosity, something which they seemed at once to contain and to conceal."[26] He could not understand what lay behind the impression, and he wanted to store it away to think about. He felt that something was concealed, "hidden behind the steeples of Martinville."[27] As he sat in the carriage on the way home, he borrowed paper and pencil from the doctor and wrote down a little account of what he had seen. In this composition he added something we have not already been told. As they left Martinville, the three steeples vanished and then returned once more, "drawing close to one another, forming now against the still rosy sky no more than a single dusky shape, charming and resigned, and so vanishing in the night."[28] They seem like "three golden pivots," "three flowers," "three maidens in a legend."[29] But nothing he thinks of them can explain his "obsession with the steeples and the mystery which lay behind them."[30] Instead of being depressed, "As though I myself were a hen and had just laid an egg, I began to sing at the top of my voice."[31]

When he arrived home, he entered once more a "zone of melancholy . . . distinct from the zone in which I had been bounding with joy a moment before."[32] Had the joy come from a perception of oneness, something that appeals to some deep longing in the human soul? And did the melancholy come from his realization that oneness is still unattainable? Whatever the reason, he reverted to being a child not able to "take my anguished eyes from my mother's face."[33]

The narrator breaks always at this point to comment on the importance of incidents like this one, belonging to the Méséglise or the Guermantes Way, importance "for the life of the mind."[34] Later in life he would think of fragments of these two landscapes, as detached as "a flowering Delos," but bearing "the image of the landscape in which I should like to live."[35] But this is not the same thing at all as the mystery encountered on the road to Martinville. And that was immediately counterpointed by a rush for comfort to his mother. Proust, who was so sure he was incapable of presence, never lets us forget that many others are capable, especially his mother, his grandmother, Swann, Robert de Saint-Loup, and Bergotte.

The incident near Martinville and what follows jumble together three quite different experiences: an ordinary mystery, a longing for protection, and a vision of the ideal landscape, which would "establish contact with my heart."[36] He would be "exposed in later life to much disillusionment,"[37] by mistaking some new person or place with an original in the two Ways. But "it was from the Guermantes Way that I learned to distinguish between these states which reign alternatively within me."[38] He would never find untroubled peace with any mistress, "since one has doubts of them even at the moment when one believes in them,"[39] compared to the solace he received from his mother's kiss or his grandmother's loving concern for his health, "whole and entire, without qualm or reservation."[40] And yet underneath, like a recurring theme of music, he would continue to wonder about the obscure pleasure that came to him in the immediacy of his vision of three steeples bobbing back and forth on the evening horizon.

The incident involving a line of trees, while looking similar at first, is quite different. Again, the narrator as a young man was riding with his grandmother and the Marquise de Villeparisis near Balbec. "We came down towards Hudimesnil, and suddenly I was overwhelmed with a profound happiness which I had not felt since Combray, a happiness analogous to that which had been given me by the steeples of Martinville. But this time it remained incomplete."[41] The trees, unlike the steeples, did not move. They "probably marked the entry to a covered driveway and formed a pattern which I was not seeing for the first time."[42] But he could not remember where he had seen such a pattern or line of trees before. It was familiar and yet new. The three old trees were like "the reality which one recaptures on raising one's eyes from the book which one has been reading and which describes an environment into which one has come to believe that one has been transported."[43]

"I looked at the three trees; I could see them plainly, but my mind felt that they were concealing something which it could not grasp, as when an object is placed out of our reach so that our fingers can only touch for a moment its outer surface, without managing to take hold of anything,"[44] as when dreaming we almost touch someone but not quite. He wonders whether he might comprehend the experience if he were alone, and whether once comprehended, "Could I at length begin to lead a true life?"[45] This is one of the consequences, one supposes, of the assimilation of mystery into one's life.

He tries to turn the mystery into a problem. "Did the trees represent something inside himself? Where had I looked at them before,"[46] in Combray or perhaps in Germany? "Were they not rather to be numbered among those dream landscapes?"[47] He tried to "penetrate the mystery of a place,"[48] tried to "put mystery back into a place which I longed to know."[49] Had he dreamed of them last night, or had he never dreamed or seen them before at all? "Did they conceal beneath their surface a meaning as obscure and as hard to grasp, as is a distant past, inviting me to probe a new thought?"[50] Or was there no hidden thought at all, just "visual fatigue"?[51] A line of trees has its own reality and stubbornly refuses to agree with any part of his speculation. And all the while he mused, the trees themselves seemed to continue to come toward him, "some fabulous apparition, a ring of witches or of Norns."[52] So he gave up, choosing "to believe that they were phantoms of the past."[53] Mystery finally reduced to an unsolved problem?

No, they continue to haunt him. He imagines the trees "waving their despairing arms,"[54] and saying, "What you fail to learn from us today, you will never know. . . . A whole part of yourself which we were bringing to you will vanish forever into thin air."[55] Perhaps it will not vanish forever, even though the message may never be learned. But he does not know this. "I was wretched as if I had just lost a friend, had died to myself, had broken faith with the dead or repudiated a god."[56] Something had happened, and he was not ready for it.

Later in life as he is returning to Paris from a sanitorium, the train stops in open country. "The sun shone upon a line of trees which followed the course of the line. These are not the same trees, the trees near Balbec, and yet he addresses them: "Trees, you no longer have anything to say to me. My heart has grown cold and no longer hears you."[57] This is as sad in its way as the lament of Meaulnes in *Le Grand Meaulnes*: "How can a man who has once strayed into Heaven ever hope to make terms with earth?"[58] Even worse than losing heaven is to stop wishing to get there. The sense of mystery has lingered on but without the obscure happiness.

Postscript

Being is presence, Being is mystery, presence is mystery. Does not all this apply to man and Being equally? Man is the image of Being. Augustine called human beings "a great deep" (*grande profundum*), and if we mean anything at all by the word "Being," it is that Being is a great deep. "If by 'abyss' we understand a great depth, is

not man's heart an abyss? For what is there more profound than
that abyss? Man may speak, may be seen by the operations of their
members, may be heard speaking: but whose thought is penetrated,
whose heart is seen into? Do not you believe that there is in man a
deep so profound as to be hidden even to him in whom it is?"[59]
"What is deeper than the human conscience?"[60] And what about
consciousness? "It is an interior hermitage, a great solitude which is
not only not passed through by anyone but also not seen."[61]

It is all very well to talk of *disponibilité*. We know people—
pastors, doctors, nurses, friends, and relatives—who would minister
to others but who have nothing much to give. There can be a
pathos in *disponibilité*. It is not enough to cry, "Give yourself," if
you do not yet have one that can meet the Augustinian test of being
a great deep. Jesus could give, I dare say, because his life was made
up of regularly alternating periods of solitude and society. He
would go away by himself, to pray, to be with the Father. The lesson in that is that to be fully human and to be a presence, a man or
woman must have some equivalent of contemplation, some experience with reflection or meditation that can give time for the inner
self to expand. A theophany is not just a noise, it is an overflowing
of a fullness of glory. Charity—love, if you prefer—is not a mechan-
ical act; it is an overflowing of carefully gathered treasure. Out of
the depths of the soul come tentative proffers of attention and help.
Out of the depths of the communion with Being itself come riches
that do not really belong to us and are not ours to withhold. There
is nothing sadder than watching a shallow soul face to face with a
grande profundum that is hurting.

That is the point, so far as the shape and image of presence goes,
of talking today of theophany. If I did not feel "epiphany" was
equally remote a word, I might settle for it. But in a time like ours
when solitude is shunned and misunderstood, when there are fewer
opportunities for the exercise of ontological sensibility, I would
think that at least we might be cautious when we speak of the
action of love. Words are easy to say, easy to define, but words
become parts of our tactics of ignorance that what is most needful is
also now what is most difficult. To be able to appreciate the hope in
"for his mercy endureth for ever," we must recognize the interior
life and power of the Lord of mercy.

NOTES

1. Marcel, "On the Ontological Mystery," in *The Philosophy of Existence*, 4.
2. Marcel, *Being and Having*, 103.
3. Buber, *I and Thou*, 3.
4. Marcel, *Being and Having*, 100.
5. Marcel, "On the Ontological Mystery," 26.
6. Marcel, "On the Ontological Mystery," 24.
7. Marcel, *The Mystery of Being*, 205.
8. Marcel, "On the Ontological Mystery," 22.
9. Marcel, *Being and Having*, 69.
10. Buber, *I and Thou*, 12.
11. Buber, *I and Thou*, 13.
12. Marcel, "On the Ontological Mystery," 26.
13. Marcel, "On the Ontological Mystery," 26.
14. Marcel, *The Mystery of Being*, 205.
15. Marcel, "On the Ontological Mystery," 25.
16. Marcel, *Being and Having*, 69.
17. Marcel, *Homo Viator*, 50.
18. Williams, *He Came Down from Heaven*; and idem, *Descent into Hell*, chap. 5.
19. Williams, *The Descent of the Dove*, vi.
20. Williams, *He Came Down from Heaven*, 88.
21. Williams, *He Came Down from Heaven*, 86.
22. Williams, *Descent into Hell*, 99.
23. Williams, *Descent into Hell*, 98.
24. Williams, *Descent of the Dove*, 37.
25. Rolle, *The Fire of Love*.
26. Proust, I, 196.
27. Proust, I, 197.
28. Proust, I, 198.
29. Proust, I, 198.
30. Proust, I, 198.
31. Proust, I, 199.
32. Proust, I, 199.
33. Proust, I, 199.
34. Proust, I, 200.
35. Proust, I, 201.
36. Proust, I, 201.
37. Proust, I, 202.
38. Proust, I, 200.
39. Proust, I, 202.
40. Proust, I, 202.
41. Proust, I, 770.
42. Proust, I, 771.

43. Proust, I, 771.
44. Proust, I, 771.
45. Proust, I, 771.
46. Proust, I, 772.
47. Proust, I, 772.
48. Proust, I, 772.
49. Proust, I, 772.
50. Proust, I, 772.
51. Proust, I, 772.
52. Proust, I, 773.
53. Proust, I, 773.
54. Proust, I, 773.
55. Proust, I, 773.
56. Proust, I, 773.
57. Proust, III, 886.
58. Alain-Fournier, *Le Grand Meaulnes*, 147.
59. Augustine, *In Ps. XVI*, 13, in *An Augustine Synthesis*, ed. Przywara, 421.
60. Augustine, *In Ps. LXXVI*, in *An Augustine Synthesis*, ed. Przywara, 421.
61. Augustine, *Serm. XLVII*, xiv, 23, in *An Augustine Synthesis*, ed. Przywara, 422.

4 | *Mystical Presence*

Mystical Presence

In the spring of 1938 I attended a course of lectures on the psychology of mysticism at the University of Fribourg. The lecturer, a Dominican, Père de Munnynck, often referred to a book by a fellow Belgian, a Jesuit, Joseph Maréchal, *Studies in the Psychology of the Mystics*, and particularly to an essay in it, "On the Feeling of Presence in Mystics and Non-Mystics."[1] I had at that time only a casual acquaintance with the writings of the mystics, mainly through anthologies and secondary sources. But I became quickly convinced by the lectures and by my reading of Maréchal that *presence* was the central theme of mysticism, and that the truth of mysticism, if it had any, would depend on the practical application of Maréchal's distinction between a judgment of reality and a feeling of presence.

It is normal for the mind to distinguish between the reality of someone one has not seen and the presence of someone one does see. Where the question of God is concerned, it is absolutely necessary to establish presence if one is to believe in God's reality at all; otherwise, it would be very difficult, if not impossible, to establish a plausible case for the reality of God. God would be only a rumor, a supposition, a wish. But the usual arguments for the existence of God do not contain reports of God's presence. It is not surprising that they convince only those who are convinced, for one reason or another, before hearing them.

The mystic has never approached God by argument, but by

55

experience, by prayer and contemplation. Listen to the sober English mystic, Walter Hilton: "We should desire always to be conscious—so far as we may—of lively inspiration of grace brought about by the spiritual presence of God within our souls. We should desire to contemplate Him constantly with reverence, and always to feel the sweetness of His love, in the wondrous nearness of His presence. This should be our life."[2] Is this not similar to Heidegger's way of thinking of Being as presence, human beings guarding the mystery of Being? I think so.

Maréchal, Thomist that he is, reminds us that the mind normally begins its activity with the phantasmata of the senses, even if there are occasions when "God presents himself to the soul setting it free from the limitations of natural knowledge."[3] But he has little to say about that liberation, doubtful as it would be to unbelievers, as he devotes his study to "the empirical feeling of presence," which he describes as "the perception of a spatialized reality," or "sensible intuition."[4] Indeed, he faces the doubters directly only as he separates intuition from hallucination, and intuition from illusion. A hallucination is "a perception without an object,"[5] and an illusion "an alteration of a real perception."[6] Maréchal's own understanding of the mind is that it is "a faculty in quest of an intuition—of assimilation with Being, Being pure and simple," although "here below in place of the One it meets with the manifold, the fragmentary."[7] Heidegger could have accepted this and Maréchal's conviction that "the human intelligence is not merely a mirror passively reflecting the objects which pass within its field, but an activity directed in its deepest manifestations towards a well-defined term, the only term which can completely absorb it—Absolute Being, Absolute Truth, Absolute Goodness."[8] I think, however, that Heidegger might, like Eckhart, have objected that Being, Truth, Goodness, however absolute, are but veils of God. Heidegger's metaphorical language about man living within the house of Being speaks in its way of the Thomistic "assimilation," which is, I take it, another way of saying living in the presence of God.

Mystics deliberately set out to "practice the presence of God." St. Teresa understood this better than most. She knew that God is present in all things even though unlearned persons had told her that God was there only by grace.

St. Teresa was a visionary. She had a vivid imagination; she once asked the other nuns to hold her down to the floor of the chapel to keep her body from levitating. At another time she saw close beside her "a most hideous little Negro gnashing his teeth."[9] She threw some holy water in his direction and he disappeared, leaving behind "a very unpleasant smell, like that of brimstone."[10] We may recall Bernini's sculpture of her special stigmata. "In his hands I saw a great golden spear, and at the iron tip there appeared to be a point of fire. This he plunged into my heart several times so that it penetrated to my entrails. When he pulled it out, I felt that he took them with it, and left me utterly consumed with the great love of God. The pain was so severe that it made me utter several moans. The sweetness caused by this intense pain is so extreme that one cannot possibly wish it to cease."[11] This is a woman who reported that for twenty years she suffered from morning sickness.

She admitted that "sometimes I am so crazed with love that I do not know what I am saying."[12] She was quite aware of the possibility that her voices and visions might be tricks of her imagination, but she was even more sure that "anyone who has had a true vision from God will detect a false one almost immediately."[13] False locutions or visions leave no results. They do not leave the soul light, do not make it quiet, do not move it to tenderness. Above all, the test of the feeling of presence is an increase of love.

St. Teresa distinguished between her visions and her sense of God's presence, a distinction that might seem too subtle to some. "If I say that I do not see Him with the eyes of the body or the eyes of the soul, because this is no imaginary vision, how then can I know and affirm that he is beside me with greater certainty than if I saw Him? If one says that one is like a person in the dark who cannot see someone though he is beside him, or that one is like somebody who is blind, it is not right. There is some similarity here, but not much, because a person in the dark can perceive with the other senses, or hear his neighbor speak or move, or can touch him. Here this is not so, nor is there any feeling of darkness. On the contrary, He appears to the soul by a knowledge brighter than the sun."[14] And then she contrasts this with her feeling of presence. "It is not like the presence of God, which is often experienced, especially by those who have the prayer of quiet and the prayer of union. It is as if when we are on the point of praying, we discover the Person to whom we were going to speak."[15] But when her confessor asked her, "Who said that it was Jesus Christ?" she replied, "He often tells me so Himself."[16]

Perhaps this is what Maréchal means when he says, "God is not satisfied merely to help us to think of him and to remind us of his presence; he gives us an experimental intellectual knowledge of this presence, the direct feeling of God's presence, the immediate presence of a Transcendent Being."[17] Is this not an experience with the ground of Being?

I am not trying to suggest that there are proofs, evidence, for presence. I wish only, like Maréchal—who did believe in God's presence—to say something about the nature of this feeling of presence. What he says that may help is that while normally the mind works through phenomena (of the senses), concept, and discussion, there are occasions when it feels the presence of something as "an echo in the sphere of our tendencies."[18] That is, "a totally indifferent object would be non-existent for us; it must have a cerain interest in our eyes."[19] Or as William James would have said, it must appear both interesting and important. Presence has an echo, but only to one who is interested. This is the opposite, phenomenally speaking, of thinking of presence as a projection. This notion is similar to a blind person's "facial vision" as described by Ved Mehta, as "my ability to perceive the sound-shadows of objects."[20] It may be the onset of what we call intimacy, of what Buber called "the between."

Just as the mystics draw analogies between the feeling of the presence of God and the feeling of the presence of another person, particularly in the dark, so we, outside their circle of belief, may be drawn to their analogies as a way of reinforcing their own understanding of the shape of presence. In the following passage from a biographical treatise by Luis de la Puente, one can easily imagine he is speaking of the presence of someone we know, as of God. "I have experienced in prayer and at other times the presence of God in divers manners. Sometimes it seems that we see God as present, not with the eyes of the body nor in a very bright light, nor merely by reasoning, but in a special way, in which the soul suddenly feels that He to whom she speaks, He who listens to her and hears her, is before her."[21] So C. S. Lewis experienced the presence of his dead wife, as "just intelligence and attention."[22] And so one can experience others who are absent but whose presence lingers, as Being lingers. "This knowledge is similar to that which one man has of another when, as they converse together, the light goes out and he remains in darkness without seeing or hearing him and speaks to him as being present with him. It is as if in darkness one should feel at once that someone is at one's side, knowing that he has goodwill and not enmity towards you."[23] Presence reverberates.

I think something like this is recorded by St. Luke after the crucifixion. The disciples on the way to Emmaus meet Jesus whom they do not recognize. He talks to them about the events of the last days; he interprets them in the light of passages from the Scriptures. They still do not recognize him. But when he breaks bread with them, they say, after he has left, "Did not our hearts burn within us as he talked to us on the road and explained the scriptures to us?"[24] It was an act, an act of communion, not talk, that had revealed his presence. It is perfectly possible to be with someone and not feel his presence, and only afterward to be aware of it. Presence may linger and the fact be recognized only in after-effects. Perhaps this is what is meant by an echo. Presence may not always be felt immediately, but at times may be delayed.

Many of the mystics had more to worry them than presence delayed. They had to learn to live with God's absence, as does any person who goes on loving someone who has gone away. After John of the Cross they called this experience of absence "the dark night of the soul,"[25] or "dark contemplation";[26] and following John of the Cross they have kept on praying by believing that contemplation is actually better off without the satisfaction of divine illumination, because it is nothing else than a secret and peaceful inflow of God which, if not hampered, fires the soul in the spirit of love.[27] The soul no longer needs to feel the pleasures of prayer and faith because its whole being has begun to be assimilated by the being of God. Evelyn Underhill summarized this well: "All these forms of the Dark Night—the Absence of God, the sense of sin, the dark ecstasy, the loss of the self's old passion, peace and joy, and its apparent lapse of lower spiritual and mental levels—are considered by the mystics themselves to constitute aspects or parts of one and the same process: the final purification of the will or the stronghold of personality, that it may be merged without any reserve in God where it was first."[28]

Of the two kinds of mystics, those who celebrate their passion for God and those who sing elegies to the cloud of unknowing or the dark night, it is the first who have most to tell us, at least initially, about presence. St. Maria Maddalena de' Pazzi was filled with perpetual fervor. Crazed with God, like St. Teresa, "she thought incessantly of God, she spoke incessantly of God, and she wrought for God incessantly. She ran through the convent crying, 'Love, love, love!' And since she could not endure this conflagration of love, she said, 'O Lord, no more love, no more love!' Once she stripped an image of Jesus and said, 'For me You shall be naked, O my Jesus, for I cannot endure your boundless virtues and perfection, I want your naked humanhood.' "[29] She may have been sex-starved; so may St. Teresa and Mechthild of Magdeburg, and Rabia, the Muslim St. Teresa. Does it matter? As St. Teresa said, "We do not pile the wood beneath the fire ourselves; it is rather as if it were already burning and we were suddenly thrown in to be consumed."[30] The metaphysician does not make use of his or her imagination, let alone sexuality, when talking of guarding the mystery of Being, but then the metaphysician does not light fires in anyone else either. And yet is the direction of his or her passion so very different? I do not know. The metaphysician is just as single-minded, just as persistent, just as ascetic.

Does the language used make a qualitative difference? What is to prevent the metaphysician from using the imagery of the Song of Songs: "Set me like a seal on your heart, like a seal on your arm, For love is strong as death, jealousy relentless as Sheol. The flash of it is a flash of fire, a flame of Yahweh himself. Love no flood can quench, no torrents drown" (8:6–7). If it sounds strange to interchange language, it may be only because we lack the fervor of the metaphysician, not that he is thinking of something different from the ecstatic. We might make contact with Heidegger or Marcel more easily if we could hear them in the words of Mechthild of Magdeburg: "Ah, Lord, if only once it happened on a day that to my heart's desire, I look on you and love, my arms around you lovingly."[31] Why should one not try to imagine one's arms around Being? Why should not the philosopher be dedicated to the pursuit of Being in the words of Rabia: "O God if I love you for fear of hell, burn me in hell. If I love you for hope of heaven, deny me heaven. If I love you for yourself alone, give me yourself."[32] Unamuno certainly could have used these words.

Unamuno would have understood immediately the relevance of this tale of Rumi, who when he knocked on the door of his beloved and was asked who he was, answered, "It is I," and was sent away. When he came back and was asked once again who he was, he answered "It is you,"[33] and was let in. As long as the philosophers think of Being as one thing and their mind as another, they will never experience it or know what to say about it. They could learn from the passion of the mystics, from their dark night and their dark contemplation.

Metaphysical Desire

Proust's biographer, George Painter, said, "Marcel learned that it is not sufficient for a great work of art to be poetic or moral: it must also be metaphysical; and the deepest theme of *A la Recherche* is the revelation of a purely metaphysical truth."[34] What is that? It is the revelation that the recovery of lost time in involuntary memory can be the most important experience of one's life. The longing for lost time and lost self may be satisfied provided one accepts this substitute for the actual lost time and actual lost self. It satisfies the longing for something ultimate, beyond any other desire, certainly beyond any imaginable achievement in the future. The Scholastic notion of a natural desire for God (or, Maréchal would say, for absolute truth, absolute goodness, absolute being) is transformed into a desire for what seems to be both unknown and unachievable, and which, if satisfied, will make the mind feel it has found all that it can possibly want. This is how Proust felt, and this is why he used metaphysical language to describe how he felt when he discovered his substitute for real presence. Proust knew no fire of love for God, and he had no metaphysical dreams about truth, goodness, or Being. He knew what it is to desire a woman, to long for a place, but it never occurred to him that the satisfaction of any particular desire would satisfy all desire. That could happen only if what he most wanted and most regretted, lost time, could somehow be recovered. Like the young Kierkegaard who longed for "a truth which is true for me, the idea for which I can live and die,"[35] Proust's ultimate would combine something he could recommend to others, but which above all defined his own existence. Others might look for something similar, but when they found it, it would be composed of the material of their own lives.

Proust had taken courses in philosophy, and the language he uses reflects that education. He probably would have agreed with Hemingway when he said, "I was always embarrassed by the words sacred, glorious, and sacrifice, and the expression in vain. Abstract words such as glory, honor, courage, or hallow were obscene beside the concrete names of villages, the numbers of roads, the names of rivers, the numbers of regiments and dates."[36] Proust himself did not hesitate to write about his own desire for "the real world," "our true life," "the true self," "the essence of things," "the idea of existence," all metaphysical terms. At the very time that Vienna, Oxford, and Cambridge were getting ready to denounce metaphysics, Proust was casually reasserting the importance of metaphysical desire.

Proust cannot be understood apart from his belief that the goal of life is to "contemplate the essence of things"[37] liberated from time. He spoke of "fragments of existence withdrawn from time," "a fragment of time in the pure state," "a minute freed from the order of time," "man freed from the order of time."[38] We read him for the enjoyment of stories of his childhood in Combray-Illiers, and for the social world of Paris before World War I. But we miss what it is all about if we do not understand that the whole novel is but an extended contemplation of life that was singularly precious and metaphysically ultimate for one man—Proust. If one starts questioning the rightness of his metaphysical language, that is to miss the point of the longing—the metaphysical desire—within his quest for lost time and lost self, and to miss the special joy in his discovery of a certain means to pull his life together. "The permanent and habitually concealed essence of things is liberated and our true self which seemed to be dead, is awakened and reanimated."[39] This cannot be taken as literal, sensuous fact. It is the only way Proust had to express the satisfaction of ultimate desire.

The language he uses is the two-world language of Platonism and Buddhism that Nietzsche scorned. But if the God who had died was the God of another world, the reality that both Proust and Nietzsche believed in was completely of this world (the landscape of Combray and the eternal recurrence). The difference between them was that Proust kept on using metaphysical language to suggest the ultimacy of his desire.

Proust believed that metaphysical desire could be satisfied by the contemplation of realities recollected involuntarily. In this respect he was as good an empiricist as any Anglo-American philosopher. But that did not mean he was against metaphysics. His view of metaphysics, like Marcel's, was that it can be concrete as well as abstract. The past cannot live again, but it can be felt again. What is felt was once actual; the feeling itself is now actual. The sense of the presence of the past is not the same as the sense of the present as present, but it may be an acceptable substitute for those who do not believe there is time enough in the present to dwell on the present and taste its essence. Proust believed that the mind does not stay long enough with anything immediately present either to see it as a whole or be sure of its special flavor. Only later, if we are given a total memory, is there time. For him contemplation is never of the present but of a reality once present that has gone through a sort of aging process in the unconscious. How different this kind of contemplation is from religious contemplation can be seen in a passage from Thomas Aquinas: "That which belongs principally to the contemplative life is the contemplation of divine truth, because this contemplation is the end of the whole human life."[40] Between contemplation of divine truth and contemplation of the past is, at least in theory, contemplation of the present.

In each kind of contemplation there is an ideal of some kind of perfection. For Proust it was "the image of the landscape in which I should like to live."[41] This is not God, but for Proust more moving than any idea of God might be. Perfection is what *I* like, or as Maréchal would say, it is what *interests* us. To Proust perfection always applies to the image of someone he desired: "a sentiment of mystery that had attached itself for me, first to Gilberte, then to the Duchesse de Guermantes, then to Albertine,"[42] and to others, Swann, his mother, his grandmother. It is the combination of an ideal of perfection and the mystery of certain persons in certain places that makes Proust unique. If this is called metaphysical, so be it. Proust's metaphysics does not require him or us to reduce experience to abstractions. No fiction is more sensuous than Proust's, more physical. Instead of pretending that transient reality only reflects timeless reality, as Plato would, he rejoices in his discovery that the real and the ideal can be one and the same. The true world and the real self turn out to be the very world that traditional metaphysics is thought to be in a hurry to get beyond. For Proust, universals and particulars are not opposed; they turn out to be the same. Swann's Way, Combray, is the ideal landscape of the soul of Proust. He cannot imagine anything higher or greater.

Proust was not an Augustine or a Heidegger *manqué*. Nor was he looking for a presence that would have satisfied St. Teresa of Avila or John of the Cross. He was not looking for a presence that would love and protect him. He had already met such presences in his mother and grandmother. He did not need God. Nor was he looking for Being. He was looking for what he had already had and lost, a self in a certain landscape. His kind of metaphysical desire was doomed to failure from the start. For it is more reasonable to hope for an experience of Being or God than to hope the past will return, except by thinking of resurrection as a phenomenon of memory.

Proust could only think that metaphysical desire had found its end by changing the end as he went along. If what is wanted is that the dead be raised, desire will fail. If one can be satisfied with a substitute reality, then desire will be rewarded. Metaphysicians typically disappoint their readers who, guided by their own longing for something absolute, have abstractions palmed off on them. Proustian metaphysics at least acknowledges the necessity of discovering a sense of reality, even if it is long gone. Proust's actual landscape is not ours, but it is nearer ours than the landscape of Plotinus or Hegel. We may say of them, "Is that all it is about?" or as St. Thomas Aquinas said of his *Summa* on his deathbed, "It's straw." But after reading Proust, we not only remember the little madeleine dipped in tea or the sunshine on a balcony or pink hawthorns or twin steeples or a little phrase of music or someone Swann loved, we are moved to remember ourselves and similar things in our lives.

To read Proust is to agree to enter a conspiracy to pretend that the sense of the past is as good as the sense of the present. But even the power of his art could not make it live again, and he knew it. The question should be whether human beings are made for immediacy or memory. The magic of Proust is that after a while this distinction becomes blurred. One feeling is no better than another because it may be more intense than the other, but because it is more real. The prisoners in Plato's cave did not know the difference between shadows and the sun. But those who have seen the sun, like the mystics or the great philosophers, do know the difference. And who would not rather be in the presence of someone alive whom he loved than in the presence of a memory of an illusion of presence? You cannot go to bed with a memory.

The Ideal of Unsatisfied Desire

Most of us give less thought to metaphysical desire than to particular desires. We want this job or that person to do this, to go there. And if we are fortunate enough to satisfy our desires, there is usually something more to want that we do not yet have. It is our lot to live with unsatisfied desires and, as one is satisfied, to try another. In Proust the story is different. As George Painter again says, "The terrible half-truth is that desire is vain not because it is frustrated but because it is fulfilled."[43] Gilberte, the Duchesses de Guermantes, and Albertine do not evade Marcel; he loses interest in them. He reaches the inner circles of the Faubourg St. Germain only to become bored with society. And when involuntary memory shows him the way to art, he loses interest in everything else. Only metaphysical desire remains, and the terms of satisfying that have had to be changed. At the moment when he ceases to strive for love or social position, the door to his vocation is opened and the door to his future closed. This, more than anything else, could explain why he looks at the daughter of Gilberte not as another chance for love but as a symbol of the past.

When he was young he had seen in Mme. de Guermantes "the charm of an historic name."[44] Society, its names and places, was a kind of poetry for him. Once it had accepted him, he saw it for what it is, shallow and malicious, like Mme. de Guermantes who has "an intelligence and sensibility closed against innovation."[45] Real people are less interesting than their poetry. They are not adequate objects of metaphysical desire. But there are moments, sometimes episodes, that "made [him] think life was worth living."[46] They take him to the threshold of metaphysical desire as neither social ambition nor preoccupation with love ever does. Someone else would find in love something unconditional; Proust did not. He could not feel of anyone what Heloise felt for the damaged Abelard: "My heart was not in me but with you, and now, even more, if it is not with you, it is nowhere."[47] He could not feel as Cathy did of Heathcliff: "He is more myself than I am."[48]

But they were recording life from across the threshold of presence and are therefore not as accessible to most of us. It seems to me that in Proust's experience of having his principal desires satisfied, without its making any difference is a lesson for us. In the first place, it taught him that particular desires do not matter after all. In the second place, it left him open and ready for the satisfaction of metaphysical desire by involuntary memory. He had not been ready for his discovery of metaphoric memory until he had come to the end of particular desire. And then he found out that metaphysical desire itself may not be satisfied in the terms he had looked for. The past could not return. The sense of presence was still not possible. But a substitute had been found, an echo from the past that would not end as one more fragment of his life, now present, then dead forever. He would be able to live within its reverberations.

There is an analogy here with Marcel's problem and mystery. When a solution to a problem is found, there is nothing more to look for. Life then becomes boring until another problem presents itself. But a mystery lingers on, as the rediscovery of the past lingers on in Proust's memory, and in Proust's art. It comes to nothing, so to speak, as, in tantric maithuna, sexual intercourse comes to nothing. The semen is not released, but nirvanic bliss is attained. Unsatisfied desire has led to a strange satisfaction of metaphysical desire. "The erotic play," says Mircea Eliade, "is realized on a transphysical plane, for it never comes to an end. They not only experience bliss but are also able to contemplate reality directly."[49] Maithuna is a metaphysical experience, much the same as Proust's involuntary memory, and is accompanied by ecstasy and joy. No wonder that Proust thought of calling the last section of his work, in which he celebrates this discovery, "perpetual adoration."

The Power of Fantasy

I have no doubt that there are no fantasies more fantastic than those of some of the mystics—not Walter Hilton but William Blake, not John of the Cross but Teresa of Avila, not Meister Eckhart but the writer of the Book of Revelation. Fantasy and mysticism are often found together, but they do not need to be. Presence is the indispensable ingredient in mysticism but not in fantasy. But there is an aspect of presence that one sometimes finds in the capacity of the mind to imagine a life different from the one it is used to and will probably continue with. That is the capacity of the mind to want to enter into the life of someone else, giving up to some degree the limits of its own life.

There is an episode in *Remembrance of Things Past* that itself lingers beyond its telling as almost no other does in that long novel. It is the story of the young man waking up on the train to Balbec at sunrise as the train slows down to halt for a few minutes at a wayside station. I was reminded by it of a crossing in South Carolina as my train sped toward Charleston, and also of a halt in the Great Karroo north of Capetown. But even without personal memories I would still see, with Proust, "some ragged clouds whose fleecy edges were of a fixed, dead pink, like the colour that dyes the feathers of a wing that has assimilated it or a pastel on which it has been deposited by the artist's whim."[50] The sky turned pink as the rail line changed directions: "a nocturnal village, its roofs still blue with moonlight, its pond encrusted with the opalescent sheen of night." The passenger runs from side to side to "collect on a single canvas the intermittent antipodean fragments of my fine, scarlet, ever-changing morning."[51]

The train stops at a little station between two hills. Below the track in a gorge with rushing water, a girl climbs up the path carrying a jar of milk and coffee. She passes along the train, from window to window. At this point the narrative comes alive as Proust describes the sunrise on her face and at the same time the sudden desire of the young man for her. "Flushed with the glow of morning, her face was rosier than the sky. I felt on seeing her that desire to live which is reborn in us whenever we become conscious anew of beauty and happiness."[52] He realizes that she attracts him not because of any general ideal of beauty that he has but because he sees her as an individual in a particular place. "This handsome girl gave me at once the taste for a certain happiness that would be realized by my staying at her side. Life would have seemed an exquisite thing to me if only I had been free to spend it, hour by hour, with her, to go with her to the stream, to the cow, to the train, to be always at her side, to feel that I was known to her, had my place in her thoughts." He calls her to bring him coffee, she starts to come, and the train moves off. "Above her tall figure, the complexion of her face is so burnished and so glowing that it was as if one were seeing her through a lighted window."[53] Then we see her go back down the path to the watch house. It is over.

But for the moment that he longed to be with her, "it was the whole of my being which confronted her."[54] Proust never says this again. In this fantasy he has been "introduced as an actor upon the stage of an unknown and infinitely more interesting universe. . . . That handsome girl was like part of a life other than the life I knew, separated from it by a clear boundary."[55] And he says that if he did not have to be separated from her, he would gladly "die to myself." But "alas, she must be forever absent from the other life towards which I was being borne with ever-increasing speed."[56] For Proust this is extraordinary; it would be hard to find a more self-enclosed man than Proust. Never again would he dream of dying to self or giving the whole of himself. But for a few moments in fantasy he wanted to. This is where an experience of presence can lead if it is allowed.

For contrast we recall other encounters with young women. A peasant girl at Roussainville? "Her kisses would reveal to me the spirit of those horizons, of the village of Roussainville, of the books which I was reading that year, and my imagination drawing strength from contact with my sensuality, my sensuality expanding through all the realms of my imagination, my desire no longer had any bounds."[57] But no peasant girl appeared. He would never embrace one in those woods, and if one had appeared would he have wanted to escape from himself?

At Carqueville he saw a tall girl sitting on the parapet of a bridge, holding in her lap a bowl of fish she had caught. "It was not only to her body that I should have liked to attain, it was also the person that lived inside it."[58] But as he stared at her, holding out a five franc piece to get her attention, the other girls standing by began to smile. End of enchantment. "This forcible appropriation of her mind had robbed her of mystery."[59]

In Paris his servant Françoise brings to his room "a slightly forward young dairymaid" to run an errand for him. "She was invested for me with that charm of the unknown which would not have existed for me in a pretty girl whom I had found in one of those houses where they attend on one." She may have been for a moment "a particle of what constitutes the eternal desire, the eternal regret of life,"[60] but he kills the desire by talking to her as master to servant. Not only does nothing in these encounters linger, he never again dreams of living with someone else, sharing a life and future he has not planned, dying to himself.

Postscript

Perhaps this is the time to recall the words of the young Wittgenstein: "It is not *how* things are in the world that is mystical, but *that* it exists. Feeling the world as a limited whole—it is this that is mystical."[61] It is said that he would say, "How extraordinary that anything should exist."[62] Heidegger felt the same, and I have no doubt so did all the mystics. But that tells us nothing much about mysticism. Even feeling the world as a limited whole says little more that is characteristic of mystics as well as philosophers, unless one associates wonder with ineffability. Those who follow the guidance of pseudo-Dionysius' *The Mystical Theology* might suppose that "mystic" means "ineffable." Dionysius writes of "the simple, absolute, and unchangeable mysteries of heavenly truth (which) lie hidden in the dazzling obscurity of the secret silence, outshining all brilliance with the intensity of their darkness, and surcharging our blinded intellects with the utterly impalpable and invisible fairness of glories which exceed all beauty."[63]

In this we see similarities with John of the Cross and *The Cloud of Unknowing*. But Dionysius' mystical theology is not gospel; it tells of transcendence but has nothing to say about immanence. He would have mistrusted immanence as much as Karl Barth did. Both retreat, glowering at everyone else, into the safekeeping of the Divine Incognito. And neither has anything to say about the presence of God. Not even Meister Eckhart's Godhead is so remote from human experience. There is always a *spark* and the possibility of a *breakthrough* into the abyss, into the ground of God. Not even God can force us to deny the power of desire and the power of fantasy to encourage souls to contemplate intimacy with some other being, woman, man, child, nature, art. Let Dionysius and Barth— who loved Mozart's music—shudder in their graves. We should trust our safety to the Christian ideal of dying to self and follow the echo of whatever good presence we may find.

NOTES

1. Maréchal, *Studies in the Psychology of the Mystics.*
2. Hilton, *The Ladder of Perfection*, chap. 41.
3. Maréchal, *Studies in the Psychology of the Mystics*, 135.
4. Maréchal, *Studies in the Psychology of the Mystics*, 98.
5. Maréchal, *Studies in the Psychology of the Mystics*, 67.
6. Maréchal, *Studies in the Psychology of the Mystics*, 68.
7. Maréchal, *Studies in the Psychology of the Mystics*, 101.
8. Maréchal, *Studies in the Psychology of the Mystics*, 100.
9. *Life of St. Teresa of Avila*, 223.
10. *Life of St. Teresa of Avila*, 223.
11. *Life of St. Teresa of Avila*, 210.
12. *Life of St. Teresa of Avila*, 281.
13. *Life of St. Teresa of Avila*, 201.
14. *Life of St. Teresa of Avila*, 188.
15. *Life of St. Teresa of Avila*, 189.
16. *Life of St. Teresa of Avila*, 189.
17. Maréchal, *Studies in the Psychology of the Mystics*, 102.
18. Maréchal, *Studies in the Psychology of the Mystics*, 82.
19. Maréchal, *Studies in the Psychology of the Mystics*, 82.
20. Ved Mehta, "Personal History," 41.
21. In Maréchal, *Studies in the Psychology of the Mystics*, 109–10.
22. Lewis, *A Grief Observed*, 57.
23. Maréchal, *Studies in the Psychology of the Mystics*, 109.
24. Luke 24.
25. John of the Cross, *Collected Works*, 297, 711.
26. John of the Cross, *Collected Works*, 366, 339.

27. John of the Cross, "The Dark Night of the Soul," in *Collected Works*, chaps. 11–20.
28. Underhill, *Mysticism*, 395.
29. de' Pazzi, *The Soul Afire*, 286–87.
30. *Life of St. Teresa of Avila*, 209.
31. de' Pazzi, *The Soul Afire*, 284.
32. Arberry, *Sufism*, 42.
33. Shah, *The Sufis*, 357.
34. Painter, *Marcel Proust*, vol. 1, 60.
35. Kierkegaard, *Journals*, 15.
36. Hemingway, *A Farewell to Arms*, 191.
37. Proust, III, 906.
38. Proust, III, 908, 905, 906.
39. Proust, III, 906.
40. Aquinas, *Summa Theologica*, "Question: The Contemplative Life," art. 4.
41. Proust, I, 201.
42. Proust, III, 1038.
43. Painter, *Marcel Proust: A Biography*, 2. 146.
44. Proust, II, 522.
45. Proust, II, 522.
46. Proust, III, 1088.
47. *Letters of Abelard and Heloise*, 117.
48. Bronte, *Wuthering Heights*, 120.
49. Eliade, *Yoga*, 267.
50. Proust, I, 704.
51. Proust, I, 704.
52. Proust, I, 705.
53. Proust, I, 706.
54. Proust, I, 706.
55. Proust, I, 707.
56. Proust, I, 707.
57. Proust, I, 171.
58. Proust, I, 769.
59. Proust, I, 770.
60. Proust, III, 137, 138.
61. Wittgenstein, *Tractatus*, 149.
62. Malcolm, *Ludwig Wittgenstein: A Memoir*, 70.
63. Dionysius, *The Mystical Theology*, 191.

5 | *Presence as Glory*

Presence as Glory

The *Iliad* opens with Achilles wasting away in grief and thinking about his *glory*. As long as he sulks in anger his *presence* will not be felt. Acceptable as this preoccupation with glory might be to Homeric heroes, it was not acceptable to the religious world of Prov. 25:27. "It is not glory to search for glory." The real glory comes from the weight and substance of presence in action, not from reputation of presence retracted. We do not admire Achilles until he returns to the battle to revenge the death of Patroklos. And we do not catch a glimpse of his presence until, after Hektor's death, he meets at night with great Priam, the father of Hektor.

Those who think of life as a long waiting for a chance to be heroic would have trouble understanding the Bible, which is one long obsession with God's presence and God's absence. The man of the Bible always stands between Moses and Job. But the Bible does not have a word for "presence." The English of Psalm 139 speaks of God's presence: "Whither shall I go from thy *presence?*" but the word is not "presence" but "face" in Hebrew and in its Greek (Septuagint) and Latin (Vulgate) translations. When Moses and Jacob are said to have met God face to face, the meaning is not that they saw God's face—"You cannot see my face; for no man can see my face and live" (Exod. 33:20)—but that they were in the presence of God. Neither part of the Bible uses abstractions such as presence, not even the Greek Parousia, which is used only for the *coming* of Christ. Of course, the Second Coming will be a presence, but that is not what is said. Heidegger's supposition that parousia was a word the early Greeks used for Being as presence may or may not be true. The Bible uses only anthropomorphic terms.

The Bible does talk of "glory," the manifestation of presence. The Hebrew word is *kabod* or *kavod*; the Greek is *doxa*. Thus, "the earth is filled with glory" (Isa. 6:3); "the glory above the heavens" (Ps. 8:1); "the King of glory" (Ps. 24:7); "the glory of thy kingdom" (Ps. 145:11); "the power and the glory" (Dan. 2:37); "the Lord of glory" (1 Cor. 2:8); "the Father of glory" (Eph. 1:17); "the glory of his power" (2 Thess. 1:9); "the brightness of his glory" (Heb. 1:3). We do not see God; we do see God's glory. Jesus' disciples saw him enter a cloud on the mount of the Transfiguration, and when he came out of the cloud, "his face shone like the sun" (Matt. 17:2). He had been near "the power and the presence" (2 Pet. 1:16).

The Bible's story of humankind begins with the forced exile from God's presence and the beginning of a return to exile through the covenant of Yahweh with Abraham. The rules of the covenant are listed in the ten commandments given to Moses on Mount Sinai. The Book of Exodus gives a paradigmatic account of a divine-human encounter, prefiguring prophetic theophanies and the association of Jesus with his disciples (from a Christian point of view).

The sons of Israel came out of the land of Egypt into the wilderness of Sinai and pitched their camp at the foot of the mountain. Yahweh called down to Moses to come up to him. "I am coming to you in a dense cloud so that the people may hear when I speak to you and may trust you always" (Exod. 19:9). At daybreak on the third day, there were "peals of thunder on the mountain and lightning flashed, a dense cloud, and a loud trumpet blast, and inside the camp all the people trembled" (Exod. 19:16) as the Baal Shem Tov trembled in Poland in the middle of the eighteenth century as he stood in the House of Prayer. The mountain was wrapped in smoke, and the whole mountain shook. Moses climbed the mountain, and God gave him the ten commandments. When Moses went down, he put the commandments in writing. But Yahweh called him up again another day to give him the commandments on stone tablets. Once more cloud covered the mountain, "and the glory of Yahweh settled on Sinai. . . . To the eyes of the sons of Israel the glory of Yahweh seemed like a devouring fire" (Exod. 24:17) as Moses went up into the cloud, where he stayed for forty days and forty nights. He stayed so long that his people apostasized. When he found them, he smashed the tablets and ordered 3,000 of his people massacred so that Yahweh would not in anger slaughter them all and break his covenant with Abraham. Then he went up the mountain once more and said to Yahweh, "Show me your glory, I beg you" (Exod. 33:15). Yahweh replied, "I will let my splendor pass in front of you, and I will pronounce before you the name of Yahweh. . . . I have compassion on whom I will, and I show pity to whom I please. You cannot see my face [but] you stand on the rock, and when my glory passes by I will put you in a cleft of the rock and shield you with my hand while I pass by" (Exod. 33:23).

This became a model for all later theophanies in the Bible, for the Transfiguration of Jesus, for mystical interpretations of Greek theologians, and for the Kabbalism of Jewish mystics. God would continue to manifest himself in cloud, thunder, fire. God would never be seen, but God's glory would be manifested in cloud, thunder, fire, and, finally, for Elijah in a whisper of a breeze. Moses, like Jesus, reflected the brightness of the Father's face, and he put a veil over his face except when he was in the presence of Yahweh. Gregory of Nyssa, in *The Life of Moses*, suggests the effect this encounter with the divine presence might have when he says, "The true vision of God consists rather in this, that the soul that looks up to God never ceases to desire him. Moses' desire is filled by the very fact that it remains unfulfilled."[1]

The glory seen by Moses, the glory manifested to Isaiah and Ezekiel, was the same glory celebrated solemnly by John in the Fourth Gospel: "The Word was made flesh, he lived among us, and we saw his glory, the glory that is his as the only Son of the Father, full of grace and truth" (John 1:14). It is the glory that accompanied the miracles of Jesus, the glory of his resurrection presence to the disciples and later to the whole Church. It is not something that can be sought, as Achilles sought his own glory. It is a manifestation of presence alone and not only comes in the darkness of people's lives but, like the direct brightness of the sun, sometimes blinds those who approach. This is how Dionysius, *The Cloud of Unknowing*, and John of the Cross understood the effects of God's presence.

The Jewish rabbinical mystics of the Kabbala (the Tradition), neither philosophers nor Talmudists, developed over centuries a cosmology and psychology about the drama of the divine life that invented words that were unknown to the Bible. The divine presence became *Shekinah*, and *Kabod* (glory) its manifestation. They thought of God as having an inner life, an I and a You, a principle of the Infinite, *Shekinah*. The work itself comes from *Sh-k-n*, the Hebrew root for "dwell." God's presence dwelt among men. And in the Fourth Gospel, the Greek verb for "*dwelt* among us" is *eskenosen*, derived from the Hebrew. The *En-Sof*, the infinity, is never revealed. It is the hidden holiness, manifested in the *Shekinah*. The hidden holiness is the Godhead, the *deus absconditus* of Isaiah, Pascal, and Barth, the principle of transcendence, the *mysterium tremendum* of Rudolf Otto. The *Shekinah* is the presence of God that is the real aim of prayer, because it is more accessible, being that part of God that is emerged with creation.

The Kabbalists believed that man's exile from the presence of God is but a reflection of God's exile from God's self, as the inner unity of God was broken up and the Shekinah—long after the inner retreat of God in *Tsimtsum*, to make room for creation—was scattered in sparks of light all over creation. It is the vocation of Israel to gather up the sparks so that God's glory can be returned to God to complete the cosmic drama (in *Tikkun*). As Gershom Scholem says, "The mystic strives to assure himself of the living presence of God, but at the same time he is unwilling to renounce the idea of the hidden God,"[2] to whom all things must return.

The Kabbalists were even bolder. They imagined the inner life of God as a marriage between masculine and feminine principles, *Shekinah* being the feminine. And some suggested that Moses had intercourse with the *Shekinah* on Mt. Sinai and thereafter did not have intercourse with his wife. This would be more offensive to some rabbis than St. Paul's suggestion that just as man made in God's image is the glory of God, so woman is the glory of man. Through contemplation on the glory of God wherever it is to be found, Kabbalist and Christian share a common view of the target of mystical contemplation: "the hidden holiness of God."

To Gerard Manley Hopkins holiness is only half hidden, and whatever is unconcealed is glorious. In poem after poem he remarks on what he called the "instress" of nature, the inner energy, the anonymous presence of God. When we see beauty in nature or in persons, we glimpse the indwelling being of God, without which not only would there be no glory, there would be no individual reality, no "inscape" or individual form. The mind may be satisfied not to probe, to be content with seeing without supposing, acknowledging beauty of form, effulgence of energy. But if not content, it can as Christian poets and theologians do— Hopkins the chief among them—penetrate the underlayment of material being to the energy of spirit, making it real, alive, or lovely.

When Hopkins says that "the world is charged with the grandeur of God,"[3] his faith connects the "greatness" of nature with "the dearest freshness deep down things."[4] And this freshness lives "because the Holy Ghost over the bent world broods with warm breast and with ah! bright wings."[5] The holiness is not hidden to faith, but it takes faith to conclude that, behind or within, "this piece-bright paling shuts the spouse Christ home, Christ and his mother and all his hallows."[6] His world is not only ontologically deep and inhabited, it is theologically and biblically inhabited as well.

This puts a strain on the unbeliever, of course. But is there anyone who cannot meet him part way below the surface? "What is all this juice and all this joy? A strain of the earth's secret being in the beginning."[7] Well, perhaps there are some who would see in this a bid for metaphysics and hold back. The "secret being" is what Rahner and Heidegger meant by "presence." It is "mystery . . . instressed, stressed."[8] Hopkins added, "For I greet him the days I meet him, and bless when I understand."[9] Change the pronoun to "it," and we can still say, "I greet it as I meet it." Faith aside, is that satisfactory? Is it even satisfactory to one who feels the need to use ontological as well as physical language? Perhaps not.

There is "glory in thunder"[10]—the prophets also thought so. It is difficult to restrain oneself from saying, "Glory," even if one stops at the edge of saying, "Glory be to God for dappled things."[11] And yet questions do break through. "What is all this juice and all this joy?"[12] Hopkins tries the nonmetaphysical mind sorely when he answers, "a strain of the earth's secret being in the beginning,"[13] when in looking at "the azurous hung hills" he sees them as, not just calls them, "*his* world-wielding shoulder, majestic—as a stallion, very violet-sweet."[14] And when he tosses us his challenge: "These things, these things are here, and but the beholder wanting, which two when they meet, the heart rears wings bolder and bolder and hurls for him, O half hurls earth for him off under his feet."[15] It is as if he, like us, is drawn as to a magnet closer and deeper within the world as presence, and in ecstasy cries, "Give beauty back, beauty, beauty back to God, beauty's self and beauty's giver."[16] The ultimate test of presence and intimacy, of nature or man and woman, is to respond by returning the gift to the giver, in words, in cries, in deeds.

For the average person, the glory of nature is probably easier to believe in than the glory of a nation. Sin and failure, flaws, mar the faces of humankind. There are, as we must acknowledge, evil presences as well as good, horror as well as glory manifested in menace and corruption. They do not dazzle, they infect and destroy.

Presence announces itself in glory. It beckons, it seduces. It is not given simply to admire but to draw us closer. In his famous university sermon, "The Weight of Glory," C. S. Lewis mentioned the choice to be made: "We can be banished from the presence of Him who is present everywhere and erased from the knowledge of Him who knows all. We can be utterly and absolutely outside—repelled, exiled, estranged, and unspeakably ignored. On the other hand, we can be called in, welcomed, received, acknowledged. We walk every day on the razor edge between these two incredible possibilities."[17] He went on to speak of "our lifetime nostalgia, our longing to be reunited with something of the universe from which we now feel cut off, to be on the inside of some door which we have always seen from the outside."[18] The Kabbalist uses myth to suggest the same possibilities. He says that we are meant to gather up the fragments of light, the sparks of Eckhart to lead the *Shekinah* back to her Master. What we see in nature and in the intimacy of love is a *radiance* that flows from the hidden powers of presence, cosmic instress. Who are we, any of us, to suppose that we can do more than try to borrow such power?

The Glory of Hawthorns

Rumors of glory from the Bible and Kabbalism may be more remote than anything else we have heard about presence. There is little that is either natural or human in the Bible to keep one from floating off into the ether. I have much the same feeling of headiness as when I meditate on Barth's *Epistle to the Romans* or Meister Eckhart's sermons. I would call them abstract except that I cannot get rid of a gnawing sense that anything people have tried to say about the majesty of God may have some truth which I with my middle-of-the-twentieth-century mind cannot quite live up to. I have never been able to dismiss history's faith in the glory of the hidden holiness as easily and contemptuously as I scorn religious sentimentality. I have not let the strictures of philosophy or literary criticism prevent me from continuing to look for traces of glory, whatever its inner texture turns out to be. That is why I find it a relief to have the ordinariness of Proust to go back to after accompanying Moses and Jesus up their mountains. For in the hawthorns of Swann's Way I can encounter with him flashes and masses of color which, compared to the winter drabness of suburb and city, warm my heart if they do not quite lift my eyes to heaven.

Proust's love of hawthorns is a case in point, and all the more interesting because he saw them as symbols of religious as well as secular desire, symbols of two parts of his life, Combray and Tansonville. In the month of May the church of Saint-Jacques was decorated with hawthorns, at the same time that the hedgerows near Swann's estate were laden with blossoms. Saint-Jacques meant church and a happy childhood; Tansonville meant the mixed desire and fear, the poignancy, of sexual love.

What orchids (cattleyas) and a little phrase of the Vinteuil sonata were for Swann, hawthorns were to Proust's little Marcel. "As Gilberte had been my first love among girls, so these had been my first love among flowers."[19] But while orchids and the little phrase are associated with eros, the hawthorns are associated with the adoration of God and His Mother as well. Marcel had first seen hawthorns on the altar of the parish church. The leaves were in the shape of a scallop shell, the symbol of St. James of Campostella and of all pilgrims. It is also in the shape of the madeleine, the biscuit dipped in tea by Proust and his mother, the incident in 1909 that set off the chain of metaphoric memory that led him to the shrine of his own quest for lost time.

The Combray brought to life by this is the Combray of the month of May, month of Mary. The child falling in love with the pink hawthorns massed around the high altar of Saint-Jacques, knows he is falling in love with much more than pink flowers. Offered by "Nature herself" they decorate "holy ground,"[20] ground of devotion of the community of believers and adornments for their perpetual adoration. Not long after seeing them in church he walked to Tansonville and entered into his lifelong adoration of girls. The entire Proustian work should be seen *à l'ombre des jeunes filles en fleur*. His subsequent obsession with sadism and homosexuality only goes to prove the norm of nature and the ideal of innocence. Proust never assumed that either sadism or homosexuality is normal. The *Recherche* begins and ends in an undisguised appreciation of feminine beauty.

Odette de Crécy's fondness for orchids and chrysanthemums sets her apart symbolically from her daughter Gilberte. Hawthorns are not hothouse flowers, and when we think of them, we think of the church and its practices as well as of Gilberte and a boy's infatuation. The day he walked along the hedgerows of Tansonville was the day he first fell in love. It was not to be an unhappy love affair like that between her mother and Swann, just an unconsummated one that would gradually fade away. But it is Gilberte's daughter to whom he is introduced when he is elderly, as a possible successor to Albertine who had been the successor to Gilberte.

Like the hawthorns encircling the park at Tansonville and the hawthorns banked against the altar, Gilberte's hair was "powdered with pink freckles."[21] Before the altar he is reminded of "springtime violence,"[22] like the "whole path throbbing with the fragrance of hawthorn-blossom, the hedge resembling a series of chapels, whose walls were no longer visible under the mountains of flowers that were heaped upon their altars; while beneath them the sun cast a checkered light upon the ground, as though it had just passed through a stained-glass window; and their scent swept over me, as unctuous, as circumscribed in its range, as though I had been standing before the Lady-altar." They "framed the stairway to the rood-loft or the mullions of the windows and blossomed out into the fleshy whiteness of strawberry flowers."[23]

This criss-crossing of the religious and the secular came easily to Proust, not because he was not religious but because as an artist he could appreciate the absence of barriers between one kind of meaning and another. In the village church the flowers are arranged with "a careless grace,"[24] another reminder of the generosity of grace, "a fragrance of bitter-sweet almonds," "gusts of fragrance . . . like the murmuring of an intense organic life."[25] This seems to me a very good way of thinking about presence itself. And it should make no difference to us whether we call it by one name or another, religious or secular.

On the festal altar the buds had opened, paler in color than on the hedgerow, but "as the bottom of a bowl of pink marble, its blood-red stain."[26] On the hedge they "glowed, smiling in fresh pink garments, deliciously demure and Catholic."[27] "For my own part, I set a higher value on cream cheese when it was pink, when I had been allowed to tinge it with crushed strawberries."[28] Eros, May, Mary, cream cheese, the heart of the artist lets his mind swing easily from one to the other. But his heart rose to an altar not first in church but at Tansonville where he felt for the first time love's mystery. He lingered there, standing still, "better to concentrate upon the flowers, the feeling they aroused in me remained obscure and vague."[29] It will take more than pink hawthorns to evoke the great mystery that only the loving presence of another person can release, to say nothing of paralysis before the King of Glory, or the brightness of the Father's face.

Again and again Proust reminds his reader that the hawthorn is a thorn bush. Its long, sharp points prick the unwary as I can personally testify. Like the thorn hedge of Sleeping Beauty, Briar Rose, inaccessible for so long, but behind which the true prince may yet find the love he has heard rumors of. Proust himself never did. I think he understood instinctively something "religious" people often seem to be blind to—that all love, even all desire, in the end, has the same source.

Exhilaration in Autumn

Each aspect of our apprehension of Being draws a different response. From presence, liberation, and renewal, from mystery, wonder, and awe, from glory, exhilaration, and praise. How rare these responses are, and none more rare than spontaneous exhilaration. Life has too many distractions, too many sources of tension to permit much spontaneity. We know what it is to feel always on guard. Besides, spontaneity needs the acknowledgment of someone or something beyond our imagining, beyond normal expectation, or else the wish to be open quickly fades into tepidity. In a world where our view of glory is superficial, where we too seldom believe in the possibility of grandeur, even in art or nature, the weights of tensions and distractions keep us from rising to any extended paean of praise.

There is a difference between the transient excitement when we see a sunset or sunrise and the exhilaration which is the expression of the whole being. Because it is increasingly rare to respond with the whole being to anything, one may not believe there can be any difference between pleasurable excitement—in sex or art—and an exhilaration that makes one relatively speechless. The "roll, the rise, the carol, the creation"[30] of a poem by Hopkins is closer than one might at first suppose, to the "stammering"[31] of John of the Cross' experience of "the unknowing transcending all thought."[32] Glory is but the manifestation of the transcendent presence, the sense of "the Holy One, Praise Be His Name."[33] The reality that we perceive, that we then judge to be greater than anything we have yet perceived or thought, has different faces but betrays the same holy power of Being. There are different faces and one Being, different voices and one Lord, the King and Lord of Glory. In the spontaneity of human response to beauty, to power, to loving acceptance beyond expectation, the inner holiness is acknowledged as grand and glorious. Our natural reaction is to sing for joy.

But I would distinguish, at this point, exhilaration from joy. I take it that even for Proust there was a difference. The joy he knew when he discovered the power of involuntary memory let him feel that he at last was participating in "the essence of things" and no longer had to fear the disappearance of his life. Joy is a feeling of communion. It is quieter, and it lasts longer. Exhilaration can be noisy and violent, and it is far less likely to signal a forgetting of the chasm between creator and creation. One cannot quite make up one's mind whether to bow down before glory or jump up and down and shout. What we call jumping or shouting for joy is what I mean by exhilaration. Joy grows on one; exhilaration is the product of sudden realization. And what is understood is different. We feel exhilarated by the power of presence (as the Baal Shem Tov jumped for the love of God), and joyful in the intimacy of presence. Religion has a place for each. Bernanos said, "Joy is the gift of the Church,"[34] the communion with the risen body of Christ. The Old Testament and especially the psalms have more to say about exhilaration. "The heavens declare the glory of God" (Ps. 19:1); "Let the heavens rejoice, and let the earth be glad, let the sea make a noise" (Ps. 96:11); "O sing unto the Lord a new song, for he hath done marvelous things" (Ps. 98:1); "O be joyful in the Lord, all you lands" (Ps. 66:1); "Praise the Lord, O my soul, thou art become exceeding glorious, thou art clothed with majesty and honor, thou deckest thyself with light as it were with a garment and spreadest out the heavens like a curtain" (Ps. 104:1–2); "O praise the Lord from the heavens, praise him in the heights, praise him, all you angels of his, praise him, all his host, praise him, sun and moon, praise him, all ye stars and lights" (Ps. 148:1–3). The psalms do not acknowledge beauty only—that is modern, and not biblical. They acknowledge the power that makes the beauty possible. Biblical exhilaration is more complex and perhaps more sustainable than the instinctive censorship that the modern mind applies to the outreach of its praise.

The difference is apparent in two incidents from Proust. The narrator as a young man is visiting his friend Robert de Saint-Loup in the barracks at Donçieres. He is given permission to sleep overnight in Robert's room. When he wakes up and looks out the window over the countryside, it was "as though from the window of a country-house overlooking the lake, shrouded still in its soft white morning gown of mist which scarcely allowed me to make out anything at all. . . . I could see only a bare hill, raising its lean and rugged flanks, already swept clear of darkness, over the back of the barracks."[35] Saint-Loup's batman brings a cup of hot chocolate. The sun breaks through the mist and exposes the russet tints of the autumn leaves. As he goes into town, past the "reds and blues of election posters on the walls . . . an exaltation raised my spirits and made me stamp, singing as I went. I could hardly keep myself from jumping in the air for joy."[36]

It is the last time that Proust's alter-ego ever responded to anything spontaneously. And we read on, five long novels further, listening to his introspective observations and reflections. We cannot call it a foretaste of his final experience of joy. It does not even measure up to the exhilaration already recorded of his solitary walks near Tansonville, Roussainville, and Montjouvain. After long hours of reading, he went out with walking stick or umbrella, and with pent-up energy released slashed the bushes as he went along. He realized that there is "a discordance between our impressions and their habitual expression."[37] I think he means that normally we do not respond with any spontaneity to our impressions but just let them come in and be forgotten. But one day, the rain over, he came to a pond and a hut with a tiled roof on which a hen was strutting on the ridge. The wind "tugged at the wild grass and the hen's down feathers. The tiled roof cast upon the pond, translucent again in the sunlight, a dappled reflection which I had never observed before, and seeing upon the water, and on the surface of the wall, a pallid smile responding to the smiling sky, I cried aloud in my enthusiasm, brandishing my furled umbrella: 'Zut, zut, zut, zut!' "[38]

Because he was Proust, he felt duty bound—so would Stendhal—to examine his spontaneity. He brought it down to the ground by supposing that "to the exhilaration which I derived from being alone would be added an alternative feeling stimulated by the desire to see appear before my eyes a peasant girl whom I might clasp in my arms."[39] If she should appear, she would add "an additional merit in everything that was in my mind, something more exalting to the charms of nature, while they in turn would enlarge what I might have found too restricted in the charms of the woman."[40] Can we believe him? It would be enough to believe with him that everywhere he went that day he imagined a "secret treasure, their deep-hidden beauty."[41]

Postscript

Glory—can we recommend it? First we have to find a world which manifests it. There is no street without hidden despair, no town without affliction, no region without its own version of oppression. In these streets, villages, and cities the cry of Job still arises: "If only I knew how to reach him, or how to travel to his dwelling" (Job 23:2). How long, how long must one wait for deliverance? Even Job's exclamation assumes the Holy One, Praise Be to Him, even if he is not listening. And yet "if I go eastward—still I cannot see him, if I seek him in the north, he is not be found, invisible still when I turn to the south. And yet he knows every step I take" (Job 23:8-9). But Job did not know the worst; that has been reserved for our time.

Buber asked the only question that can be asked now. "How is a life with God still possible in a time in which there is an Auschwitz? The estrangement has become too cruel, the hiddenness too deep. One can still believe in the God who allowed these things to happen, but can one still speak to him? Can one still hear His word? Dare we recommend him to the Job of the gas chambers? Call to him, for He is kind, for his mercy endureth forever?"[42] Buber's answer is that what saved Israel was that it experienced these contradictions as theophany. A God who bellowed and bullied, who told Job how big God is and how small man is. Some theophany. In the gas chambers, is it time to talk of the power and the glory? How dare anyone say that? It makes as much sense as Dmitri Karamazov's silly claim that there is beauty in Sodom, but is more offensive to the dignity of man.

"Whither shall I go then from thy Spirit? or whither shall I go then from thy presence? If I climb up into heaven, thou art there; if I go down to hell, thou art there also (Ps. 139:7-9). In hell? In the concentration camps? "Even there also shall thy hand lead me, and thy right hand shall hold me" (Ps. 139:10). In the absence of glory, what is left to allow anyone to say this psalm honestly? If there were a presence, even without manifestation of power and glory, if there were someone else to go down to hell with one, then might there be communion in that presence? Is it credible that the hidden one, the Holy One, Praise be His Name, might be humble enough to accompany a man, a woman, a child, on a terrible journey, power and glory forgotten? If there is an answer, it might be in something like this. Glory is reserved for a world that does not know the terrors of oppression. The power that oppresses is too near for the victim to believe in a presence that liberates until it is willing to share the suffering. That would truly be an exercise in presence: exchange and substitution.

NOTES

1. Gregory of Nyssa, *From Glory to Glory*, 55.
2. Scholem, *Jewish Mysticism*, 12.
3. Hopkins, "God's Grandeur."
4. Hopkins, "God's Grandeur."
5. Hopkins, "God's Grandeur."
6. Hopkins, "The Starlight Night."
7. Hopkins, "Spring."
8. Hopkins, "The Wreck of the Deutschland," stanza 5.
9. Hopkins, "The Wreck of the Deutschland," stanza 5.
10. Hopkins, "The Wreck of the Deutschland," stanza 5.
11. Hopkins, "Pied Beauty."
12. Hopkins, "Spring."
13. Hopkins, "Spring."
14. Hopkins, "Hurrahing in Harvest."
15. Hopkins, "Hurrahing in Harvest."
16. Hopkins, "The Leaden Echo and the Golden Echo."
17. Lewis, *The Weight of Glory*, 18.
18. Lewis, *The Weight of Glory*, 18–19.
19. Proust, I, 984.
20. Proust, I, 121.
21. Proust, I, 153.
22. Proust, I, 123.
23. Proust, I, 150.
24. Proust, I, 121.
25. Proust, I, 123.
26. Proust, I, 153.

27. Proust, I, 153.
28. Proust, I, 152.
29. Proust, I, 151.
30. Hopkins, no. 53, in *Poems and Prose*.
31. John of the Cross, "Spiritual Canticle," stanza 7, in *Collected Works*, 713.
32. John of the Cross, "Stanzas Concerning an Ecstasy," in *Collected Works*, 718.
33. Scholem, *Jewish Mysticism*, vii.
34. Bernanos, *Diary of a Country Priest*, 212.
35. Proust, II, 78–79.
36. Proust, II, 79.
37. Proust, I, 169.
38. Proust, I, 169.
39. Proust, I, 169–70.
40. Proust, I, 171.
41. Proust, I, 171.
42. Buber, *At the Turning*, 61–62.

6 | *Living Presence*

Living Presence

There are persons whom we cannot think of except as being alive. They seem to resist destruction, even when dead. It is almost as if we learn by knowing them how to define a living presence. Indeed, we want to say that there is no presence unless it is living. What is meant by this is, perhaps, a kind of emanation of character that has the power to define our own character. Around them, even remembering them, whether away for a while or permanently, we feel the whole world a more vibrant as well as more interesting place.

To say this less abstractly, I have in mind two opposite kinds of people, the brooding presences that haunt themselves and other people and the healing presences that transform those they touch. Dostoevsky knew more about the former than the latter, although I am sure he hoped he could portray the latter. Rogozhin is more real than Myshkin, Ivan than Alyosha. *The Idiot* is held together somehow by the sense the reader and Myshkin have that everywhere one goes the eyes of Rogozhin are following. Perhaps Dostoevsky meant one to think that Rogozhin is drawn to Myshkin as the demonic were drawn to Jesus. But Myshkin has no mystery, and he amuses or irritates instead of quieting. He is not crucified by the world; he collapses inwardly.

From the moment he got off the train at St. Petersburg, Prince Myshkin has had a feeling that someone's eyes are watching him.

Someone's are—Rogozhin's; he is a violent, brooding, and unhappy young man whose passion for a flawed beauty, Nastasya Filippovna, will destroy her, the prince, and himself. He single-mindedly pursues her. Myshkin is "available" to everyone and to no one. He is a Christ without an inner connection with the Father. He sees in Nastasya Filippovna's face not only extraordinary beauty and "some mystery hidden,"[1] but an unhappy nature that no one can make right. "There was a sort of immense pride and scorn, almost hatred, in that face, also something trusting, something wonderfully good-natured . . . that dazzling beauty was quite unbearable, the beauty of that pale face, those almost hollow cheeks and burning eyes, a strange beauty."[2] No Christ himself, the only thing Myshkin can think of doing for her is to offer to marry her; this is always his ideal of compassion. She reverences him, and runs away from him with Rogozhin who kills her.

Rogozhin's eyes haunt. He is an obsessive presence, emanating violence and desire, but doomed to bear the message of unreason, immune to salvation. The Prince cannot heal him, only go mad beside him. How different were the eyes that John of the Cross were wounded by: "When you looked at me, Your eyes imprinted Your grace in me; for this you loved me ardently; and thus my eyes deserved to adore what they beheld in you."[3] Rogozhin is not only graceless, he wants to possess this woman so much that his desire turns to malice. The prince has one power that is a sign of some degree of presence: he can foresee the worst that can happen to people he meets. He is a very disquieting imitation of Christ to have around. He says to Rogozhin, "You'll hate her bitterly for having loved her so much now."[4] He could not understand how a woman who could arouse so much pity in himself could arouse any desire in anyone else. "It aroused suffering, it cast a spell over your whole soul."[5] But then Myshkin did not know what it is to desire. He is like other pure characters in Dostoevsky, Alyosha, for example, whom we find it difficult to believe in.

It is easier to believe in brooding, twisted souls like Svidrigailov, Raskolnikov, Ivan Karamazov, Stavroguin. Except for Raskolnikov, whose "resurrection" we may not believe in easily either, they will collapse from the weight of the walls enclosing them. But while they live, their negative presence challenges other people's need to affirm their own sources of salvation. In the end, when we compare them to the half-presences such as Myshkin, we may conclude that there is not much difference.

At one point in *The Idiot* when Myshkin once again feels he is being followed by "those two eyes, the same two eyes,"[6] he has an epileptic fit and experiences an illumination; "a blinding inner light flooded his soul."[7] If the sight of a man in a fit "fills many others with absolute and unbearable horror which has something mystical about it,"[8] one may be tempted to liken it, as Dostoevsky does, to "dazzling light, great calm, full of serene and harmonious joy and hope"[9] or, more expansively, full of understanding and knowledge of the final cause, fullness, reconciliation, fusion. But something is missing. Not only has the illumination been prompted by disease, it is an exercise and display of pure emotion, representing the inner cosmos of the mind, and has nothing to say about God or the world. Feeling "an intense heightening of awareness," Dostoevsky himself could say on Myshkin's behalf, "Yes, I could give my whole life for this moment."[10] And yet even he knew that was not good enough. He knew one could not live within and for the self alone. In each of his novels he portrayed tortured souls living all the time on the verge of some momentous hour that would determine everything. But why? Without an inner life beyond blinding intuitive flashes, without a love to watch over them or to draw them out, they are all doomed to despair. They live with exaggerated hopes, hyperbole about each other such as Myshkin's astonishing words—meant to be compassionate—to Nastasya Filippovna: "Everything about you is perfection."[11] These are not the sober words of a Christ, but the exaggerations of a would-be lover, which he tries to erase by saying, "I'm ready to die for you."[12] "I'll look after you. I shall respect you all my life."[13] At least these words moved her to reply, "No one has ever spoken to me like that,"[14] and she went down on her knees before him. Later Rogozhin murdered her, and the prince and he lay down beside the corpse to keep watch. Myshkin, having stroked her hair and face "as though she were a little child,"[15] "so now he passed his trembling hand gently over Rogozhin's hair and cheeks as though caressing and soothing him."[16] But Myshkin's hands feel more than his mind does. Dostoevsky's Christ-like figure had not died and become entombed; he had become a real idiot.

I think Dostoevsky knew that there is a difference between Christ and Myshkin. I am not sure that he knew what it is. The Dutch theologian Edward Schillebeeckx does. The most original part of his exegesis of the Gospels is his suggestion that Jesus' "Abba-experience"[17] was the source of his "message, ministry, and praxis."[18] In Jesus' use of the ordinary secular Aramaic word *Abba* for one's earthly father, we can imagine something of his deep intimacy with God. Could this be the human clue to the mystery of this unique person, whose influence on so many exceeded what he actually said to them? Wherever he went, the sick were healed, testifying to the power of the father. Jesus' affirmation of forgiveness and salvation came out of his own familiarity with the immediacy of God, not the King of glory but the father of mankind. The *now* this man lived in was not the blinding light of an exploding consciousness, not a moment of borderline ecstasy or intellectuality, but an achievement of presence. The Word was made flesh and dwelt among them. *En-sof* and *Shekinah* were joined together unbreakably. Nourished by the constant practice of living in the presence of his Abba-consciousness, Jesus' own presence was life-giving. After Jesus, God would never again be thought of as an oppressive tyrant, full of anger, but full of kindness and long-suffering, a God whose quiet power could liberate imprisoned minds and bodies.

Schillebeeckx raises a final question. Granted that Jesus had an Abba-experience, was it after all only an illusion, "the grand illusion of his life?"[19] Or "could this person have been right?"[20] The answer surely is the same as the one Jesus himself gave to John's disciples: "Go back and tell John what you hear and see: the blind see again, and the lame walk, lepers are cleansed, and the deaf hear, and the dead are raised to life, and the Good News is proclaimed to the poor; and happy is the man who does not lose faith in me" (Matt. 11:4–5).

Who has not puzzled over the stories of the healing miracles in the Gospels? What happened? Could they have happened? Those who saw them and those who wrote about them do not give us cxplanations. Should they? All they tell us is that Jesus said things, did things, and then they were cured: things such as, "Pick up your bed and walk" (Matt. 9:6); or "Stretch out your hand" (Matt. 12:13); or "Go wash in the pool of Siloam" (John 9:7); or "Get up" (Luke 7:15); or "Come out" (John 11:43). No uniformity there. Sometimes all he said was "Be cured!" (Luke 5:14).

We are told that his teachings had authority, the authority of the fact that they were healed. We are told that "all who touched him were cured" (Matt. 14:36). But many were cured whom he had not touched. Speak or not speak, touch or not touch, nothing in common. He himself said, "It is the father living in me that is doing this work" (John 14:10), the Abba-father, the intimate father he communed with. Was not that the source of life and health? It is all very elusive for us, but not so elusive as not to defy most skeptics even today. They may say, "Well, I grant you something probably happened, but what?" They say, "Psychosomatic, perhaps?" That does not take us very far either; it is just more jargon for the unknown. All we know is that when he was present, things happened, good things, except to the envious who would hound him to death. It does look as if his being and person, call it presence in time, had a power of life that created its own witnesses in the shape of the healing of wounded souls and damaged bodies. You want to know what presence is? Try reading the Gospels again. That, I think, is what it would be like to be in the presence of someone who was present to us and not just brooding over us. Plotinus would have said that there were emanations, Maréchal echoes. Such energies do not die.

Withdrawal from Life

We do not have words to distinguish between being alive and feeling alive, being real and feeling real. And if one has never felt the difference, it may look like quibbling, a banality, a truism, to claim that there are times and occasions when we feel as if we have come to life. Not everybody alive is present to others all the time, and some may not seem present at any time. There is nothing easier or more usual than going through day after day of anticipated routines without feeling the sharpness of being alive. It is much easier to recognize when something happens than to define. I would say that most of the time we are for all practical purposes withdrawn from that sharpness of being, and only at rare intervals does one suddenly realize the distinctive tension of being alive. It is as if a machine were just quietly turning over, when suddenly it speeds up with almost unbearable acceleration and the pitch of its whine becomes almost excruciating to the hearing.

There are also moments, in memory and in dreams, when, having long become used to not feeling alive, we remember with despair that we have lost. Life has cruel moments when, having attained the safe place where we cannot any longer be hurt by the sharpness, even the pains, of being alive, we experience that odd combination of feeling alive and feeling lost that is found in men and women who have never had the good luck to live with a good presence.

For a very few of these there is sometimes reserved a little vision of what might still be, if one were adequate to it or, rather, if one had courage to dare life all over. There is poignancy in such a prospect, for one knows he will not dare. Even poignancy is better than accepting the dullness of being almost dead.

A Lost Eurydice

No proof of presence convinces more certainly than the finding of love after all hope has been lost. Nothing restores a sense of being alive less ambiguously than the rebirth that follows the appearance of the unexpected, the finding of a person who one did not know one loved so much. This means that to feel alive one needs to fear the disappearance of someone else who was alive. This is why people come alive momentarily, by contrast, at the death of loved ones. The father of the prodigal son probably never felt as alive as when his son returned.

Swann did not know he loved Odette until he thought he had lost her. His sense of his own self suddenly became charged with a unity and a purpose—to find her, to possess her—that made him an entirely different person. He had been interested in her only as a reminder of a face in a painting by Botticelli, and he was no more interested in seeing her than he would have been in seeing that painting.

But one evening he arrived at the Verdurins' late, where he took it for granted that she would be waiting for him. She had already gone, leaving a message that she would stop off at Prévost's for a cup of chocolate. When Swann did not find her at Prévost's or at any other cafe on the boulevards, he suffered "a moment of illumination, like a man in a fever who awakes from sleep [and] perceives how foreign to his nature were the thoughts that had been revolving in his mind, how novel the heartache from which he was suffering, but of which he was only now conscious. . . . He was no longer the same man, was no longer alone even . . . a fresh personality was thus conjoined with his own, life had seemed somehow more interesting."[21] He had begun to come alive, even before he found her, indeed, when he thought he would not find her. Presence not yet experienced, the image of presence withdrawn, was enough to transform his sense of his own being.

Swann's coachman advised him to give up and go home, but "he brushed past all these dim forms, as though among the phantoms of the dead, in the realms of darkness, he had been searching for a lost Eurydice."[22] It is a curious choice of an image for Odette. Swann himself was no Orpheus and once he found Odette in the darkness of the boulevards, he would never lose sight of her again. In his "moment of deprivation" he discovered for the first time "an anxious torturing need, whose object is the person alone, an absurd irrational need . . . the insensate agonizing need to possess exclusively."[23] And some cosmic machine responded. He collided with Odette coming from the opposite direction. She had been in the Maison Dorée all the time, and he had failed to see her when he looked in. His happiness which he had always theoretically believed in, now exploded with a "truth whose radiance dispelled like a bad dream the loneliness he had so dreaded."[24]

Those who feel alive give off a radiance, the inner being of which is a rebirth of energy. Proust did not record this rebirth as happening in a moment of stillness, but we can imagine stillness as its inner space, "the still point of the turning world." The moment of transformation is as pure and impassioned as any other experience of the *vita illuminativa*. The moment is pure enough, but Swann's new love is not. No love described in fiction was ever more selfish. He wants her for himself, as much of her as he can get. Neither he nor she ever considers a totally unselfish act of love. Nevertheless, there is here a simulacrum of conversion of being, from indifference to obsession, but not from emptiness to fullness of giving. Swann is paid off by a night of love making, the kind that does not know the difference betwen sex and love. He will say later that he has wasted his life on a woman who is not even his type. Proust had, however, chosen the right word to mark the dispelling of the shadow of indifference and the illumination of the soul by the discovery of the goal of its heart. He likens the scene on the boulevards that night to a scene out of Hades and to that of a traveller at the Mediterranean shore who, arriving in glorious weather, is no longer certain of the existence of the lands he has left behind as he is "dazzled by the *radiance* streaming towards him from the luminous and unfading azure of the sea."[25] He has come alive only to live to wish he were dead.

Dreams of a Traveller

I do not know which is worse: to remember real love lost or to remember the deceptions of a love that was never real. Swann lives to forget his unhappiness with Odette, and then lives on to remember it all over again. He is the kind of man who will never know presence but will be given a chance to feel something of one of the marks of presence—a new life. The life he felt was, however, only his own. He and Odette had no capacity to share anything of themselves. He wanted to possess her; she wanted his social position and his possessions. Out of that can come nothing good, only frustration of the possibility of one life expanding into the inner space of another.

Swann often dreamed of breaking off from Odette, to relieve his obsession over a woman he might own but not possess. One night he dreamed that he was at a railway station in Paris, "leaning from the window of the train towards a young man on the platform who wept as he bade him farewell, trying to persuade this young man to come away also. The train began to move, he awoke in alarm, and remembered that he was not going away, that he would see Odette that evening and the next day and almost every day."[26] Swann realized from inside the dream that he was both the traveller and the young man on the platform. One part of him wanted to break with

Odette, the other part was in terror that they might be parted. He now saw that "his love extended a long way beyond the province of physical desire; Odette's person, indeed, no longer held any place in it."[27] His love had become a malady no longer operable.

One night at a musicale at Mme. de Sainte-Euverte's, as he listened to the music of Vinteuil, he recalled the sorrows of his life and "remembered the gasjets being extinguished along the Boulevard des Italiens where he had met her against all expectations, along the errant shades on that night which had seemed to him almost supernatural."[28] He then thought that he had once belonged to "a mysterious world to which one never may return again once its doors are closed."[29] He saw himself "standing motionless before that scene of remembered happiness, a wretched figure who filled him with such pity because he did not at first recognize who it was. It was himself."[30] But he had once, in that mysterious world, been alive, and now he pities the figure that, having thought itself alive, had gone on to feel it had all been an illusion.

Not long after this, "in the twilight of a dream,"[31] he found himself walking with friends, Mme. Verdurin, Dr. Cottard, a young man in a fez "whom he failed to identify,"[32] the painter, Odette, Napoleon III, and the narrator's grandfather. They walked along a path by the sea. Odette looked back at him "with eyes welling with affection, ready to detach themselves like tears and fall upon his face, and he felt that he loved her so much that he would have liked to carry her off with him at once."[33] She said, "I must go," and left him. "He would have liked to follow her . . . his heart was frantically beating, he felt that he now hated Odette. He would gladly have gouged out those eyes which a moment ago he had loved so much."[34] The painter told Swann that Napoleon III had followed Odette. "They had obviously arranged it between them . . . she is his mistress."[35] The young man burst into tears. Swann tried to console him by saying, " 'After all, she's quite right. I've advised her to do it a dozen times. Why be so distressed?' So Swann reasoned in his dream with himself, for the young man whom he had failed at first to identify was himself."[36] He had once said, "People don't know when they're happy. One is never as unhappy as one thinks."[37] The truth of these dreams would seem to be the opposite. One is more unhappy than one thinks. He had never really known what it is to be alive. It is not that life has been withdrawn; only the prospect has been withdrawn.

We meet Swann once more near the end of his life when he knows he is dying of cancer and tries to tell his friends the Duc and Duchesse de Guermantes as they prepare to set off for a party. They do not want to hear any unpleasantness and, while unwilling to linger a while to talk to him, at the last minute tarry long enough for the Duchesse to replace her black shoes with red ones to match her dress. Swann makes it easy for them by saying, " 'I mustn't make you late' . . . because he knew that for other people their own social obligations took precedence over the death of a friend."[38] But friendship of this kind could not let him feel as music once had, that "he was no longer in exile and alone."[39]

Final Crossroads

The place Swann had arrived at may not seem much to boast of, but many people never arrive there at all. If one had been looking forward on his behalf much earlier, one would have hoped for a more active presence in the world. Swann never became more than a rich man about town, intelligent, sensitive, but essentially passive. His story is the story of a man without a future. So when he reaches the verge of death and feels for the first time no longer alone, he has reached the limit of Proust's own idea of a future. Since man is the creature who cannot emerge from himself and exists alone, Swann in a sense broke the bank when he felt that he was no longer in exile. He had always been too intelligent to be able to imagine that even friendship could change that. What had changed was that he discovered that he could still show consideration for the weaknesses of his friends, the Guermantes. For Swann this was almost an act of love.

At the end of the novel, long after Swann's death, the narrator, himself now elderly, attends a reception at the Princesse de Guermantes' (the nouveau riche Mme. Verdurin). Everyone we know is there except Swann, Robert de Saint-Loup, who was killed in the war, Albertine, who had died in an accident, and Charlus, whom he had just met outside in the street. Most of the old friends have been changed by age, and are now almost unrecognizable. Gilberte,

Saint-Loup's widow, now looks like her own mother, Mme. Swann; and Odette is now the Duc de Guermantes' mistress. Gilberte offers to introduce the narrator to a few sympathetic young women. He himself thinks that "a little amorous dalliance with a young girl in bloom would be the choice nutriment"[40] for his old age, and he "yearned once more for what I had dreamed at Balbec."[41] He wishes that "by a miracle the door might open and through it might enter not just Albertine but my grandmother."[42] He had no interest in seeing more of Gilberte, his first love, but admits that he would "always enjoy being invited to meet young girls, poor girls if possible, to whom I could give pleasure by quite small gifts, without expecting anything in return save that they should renew within me the dreams of the sadnesses of my youth."[43] Now there is "an aesthetic element in the egotism which attracted me to beautiful women who had the power to make me suffer."[44] Once this aesthetic element had been a sense of mystery, gateway to dreams of the unknown and an unknown way of life. But the unknown had become too familiar and too painful.

At this point Gilberte says, "Let me fetch my daughter for you. I should so like to introduce her to you. I am sure that she will be a charming little friend for you."[45] The reader cannot help recalling that Gilberte is the daughter of the most famous courtesan of the time and is now talking like a procuress. But Marcel thinks only of the many lines of his past that have converged in this child. "Was she not like one of those star-shaped crossroads in a forest where roads converge that have come, in the forest as in our lives, from the most diverse quarters?"[46] Radiating from her are "the two great Ways themselves,"[47] Swann's Way through her mother who is Swann's daughter and the Guermantes Way through her father, Robert de Saint-Loup, who is the nephew of the Guermantes. "And between these two high roads a network of transversals."[48] Marcel's whole life, his childhood, loves, friendships had been a "prolongation of the two ways starting out in Combray and converging in this girl."[49] He now understands that not only is life made up of what we call coincidences, but in the end nothing is irreconcilable. He says he is less impressed by "mysterious threads broken by life"[50] than by "life perpetually weaving new threads which link one individual and one event to another."[51] But all he has in mind is threads in a "rich network of memories,"[52] not new threads of a new life.

When he looks at young Mlle. de Saint-Loup, he sees her not as a living person but as a figment of time, not "time colourless and inapprehensible,"[53] but a time that had "materialized itself in this girl, moulding her into a masterpiece."[54] Just as Swann could only see in Odette a painting of Botticelli, so Marcel sees in Mlle. de Saint-Loup only another Guermantes. "She had deep-set piercing eyes, and a charming nose thrust slightly forward in the form of a beak and curved, perhaps not in the least like that of Swann, but like Saint-Loup's. . . . I thought her very beautiful; still rich in hopes, full of laughter, formed from those very years which I myself had lost, she was like my own youth."[55]

She says nothing, and we do not know her first name. If she has hopes, Marcel no longer does. A moment of the future has come and gone. He will end his life with a brief encounter with the possibility of the future, but he has less interest in a future now than ever before, not because he is nearer death but because he has discovered a substitute for both future and present in his metaphoric glimpse into the past. He knows as well as we that he will never live with a presence that would burn him with a radiant, living fire of love. He has wasted his entire life on the threshold of the possibility of presence, never willing to give and too shut up inside himself to receive.

Postscript

I sometimes think that it is easier to talk about God than about human beings. And yet whatever we say about God, we must have learned from ourselves. The God of Israel differed from the gods of other peoples as a living God does from fabricated idols. Do we understand what that means? What it means to be alive? Anything that lives differs from the inert as something that moves itself. When we think of ourselves, and even more of those we meet, it is the degree of spontaneity that we recognize behind the façade of faces, speech, and actions. If we sense a mystery in anyone else, we are thinking of the power undisclosed behind the manifestations of spontaneity that we do see, the hidden life revealed. Life is a combination of incalculable, almost unconditional spontaneity. The more enclosed a person, encumbered, self-isolated, self-centered, selfish, the less we experience the unconditional or the spontaneous. When we speak of God as the living God, we are making reference to a reality that is an ideal for us.

The tree of life, planted by the living God, was meant to be tended by a living Adam. He, shutting himself off from God, had to be content with the more uncertain, even dubious fruit of the tree of the knowledge of good and evil. In exile he would learn to cry: "My soul is athirst for God?" (Ps. 42:1); "In thy presence is the fullness of joy" (Ps. 16:11); "In him was life, and the life was the light of men" (John 1:4). The myths have been mixed here on purpose: the promise of the first man, rejected, the hope of the new man to be acknowledged.

A life that lives for itself, using its spontaneity only within its own bounds, makes no difference to the world. Whenever we sense a spontaneity that rejoices in breaking through the bounds, we may hope that its first act will be to listen to us before trying to impose itself on us. Real living is defined more by listening than by speaking, and the living God by his mercy more than by his indignation. Does she really hear us, we ask? Do I really hear her? Or has something been kept in reserve, secretive and evasive? Nothing is simpler than to thwart the extension of life's spontaneity, to give imitations of giving which are no more than pretenses of openness. Lying is meant to protect life from fully appearing, and we know enough from experience to be on the lookout for it. But to protect ourselves we deceive in return, even if only by keeping some part of us in reserve.

Nevertheless rare is the person who is not athirst for a living person, feeling that in the presence of such a one, he or she will become fully alive. Presence and Opening, recommended Heidegger, the more open the more present. The more we hear, the more we open, until the dazzling obscurity of the secret silence is manifested. The *grande profundum* does not become less deep, the hidden does not become less unknown: it cannot be exhausted. "Real life is meeting,"[56] says Buber, the meeting of one deep with another, one willingness to open itself to another self. The hidden vibrations manifest themselves as "intelligence and attention."[57]

That is the fullness of life. The rest is the infinite variety of personal contingency and resource. If there is joy, it is because there is variety as well as openness.

Not all variety leads to joy. The principle of freedom and spontaneity that Thomas Aquinas regarded as the touchstone of life has a darker side, unpredictability, something he said nothing about. We are, if not more familiar, at least more concerned than he about mood swings in the human personality. It is one thing to exalt the capacity of human beings to be more than they can imagine, to feel, to think, to say, to do what one did not know possible. There can be great satisfaction in that, provided one does not lose touch with the sense of the familiar which is the sign of identity. It is when one seems to be looking at a change of personality, when the person one sees can no longer be either recognized or counted on, that freedom and spontaneity show a troubling side.

To speak of man as a *grande profundum* is to be thinking first of all of the human being as having an apparently infinite resource for adaptation, if not change. This is the source of the glories—and, alas, of the corruption—of the imagination. How tempting it is to emphasize one option instead of its opposite. What Augustine called the "deep," what modern psychologists call the "unconscious," is so great that for the most part it is unknown, therefore, incalculable, therefore unpredictable. There is nothing wrong with unpredictability as such, until it looks as if the personality has become detached from what has been known, from the expected and familiar. I almost said, from what we have counted on.

Here too there can be ambiguity. What a relief at times to find that one no longer has to count on someone being unpleasant or, for that matter, unpredictable. To be a *grande profundum* means that the future as well as the present is to some extent always out of sight. And yet, there would be nothing more scary if that is all one can say of a person. What one needs and looks for in another is above all constancy and dependability, a stable moral identity. We want to be able to count on someone. The other side of this, the inside, is that we ourselves do have a capacity for commitment and fidelity, a prolongation of our presence in the world.

A human being is more than a great deep; he or she is a great paradox as well. No one knew this better than Pascal. For freedom means the possibility of happiness and misery, of good and evil, of commitment and of breaking out. The practical question is what kind of balance can be found to avoid destroying others and ourselves.

In a lyrical passage in *The Magic Mountain*, Thomas Mann asks again and again, "What is life?" He answers, in part, "It was warmth generated by a form-preserving instability, a fever of matter, which accompanied the process of ceaseless decay and renewal. And life? Was it perhaps only an infection, a sickening of matter, just as disease in the organism was an intoxication, a *heightening*?"[58] Let us recall Rogozhin's feverish obsession with Nastasya Filippovna and Prince Myshkin, and Myshkin's own preternaturally heightened consciousness. Both were diseased. But their heightening was an imitation of life, not life. The difference, therefore, is not to be found in the intensity, but in the achievement of balance, between stability and change, self-preservation and self-giving. This is the great achievement of the *grande profundum*.

NOTES

1. Dostoevsky, *The Idiot*, 107.
2. Dostoevsky, *The Idiot*, 107–8.
3. John of the Cross, "Spiritual Canticle," stanza 23, in *Collected Works*.
4. Dostoevsky, *The Idiot*, 245.
5. Dostoevsky, *The Idiot*, 263.
6. Dostoevsky, *The Idiot*, 267.
7. Dostoevsky, *The Idiot*, 258.
8. Dostoevsky, *The Idiot*, 268.
9. Dostoevsky, *The Idiot*, 259.
10. Dostoevsky, *The Idiot*, 259.
11. Dostoevsky, *The Idiot*, 170.
12. Dostoevsky, *The Idiot*, 196.
13. Dostoevsky, *The Idiot*, 201.
14. Dostoevsky, *The Idiot*, 201.
15. Dostoevsky, *The Idiot*, 616.
16. Dostoevsky, *The Idiot*, 657.
17. Schillebeeckx, *Jesus*, 257–71.
18. Schillebeeckx, *Jesus*, 266.
19. Schillebeeckx, *Jesus*, 270.
20. Schillebeeckx, *Jesus*, 270.
21. Proust, I, 249.

22. Proust, I, 252.
23. Proust, I, 252.
24. Proust, I, 253.
25. Proust, I, 253.
26. Proust, I, 385.
27. Proust, I, 336.
28. Proust, I, 377.
29. Proust, I, 377.
30. Proust, I, 377.
31. Proust, I, 377.
32. Proust, I, 411.
33. Proust, I, 412.
34. Proust, I, 412.
35. Proust, I, 412.
36. Proust, I, 412.
37. Proust, I, 386.
38. Proust, I, 618.
39. Proust, I, 378.
40. Proust, III, 1036.
41. Proust, III, 1036.
42. Proust, III, 1037.
43. Proust, III, 1037.
44. Proust, III, 1038.
45. Proust, III, 1084.
46. Proust, III, 1084.
47. Proust, III, 1085.
48. Proust, III, 1085.
49. Proust, III, 1086.
50. Proust, III, 1086.
51. Proust, III, 1086.
52. Proust, III, 1086.
53. Proust, III, 1088.
54. Proust, III, 1088.
55. Proust, III, 1088.
56. Buber, *I and Thou*, 11.
57. Lewis, *A Grief Observed*.
58. Mann, *The Magic Mountain*, 285.

7 | *Real Presence*

Real Presence

The Catholic doctrine of the Real Presence tested the credulity of millions of pious people for a long time. I know of no stranger historical phenomenon. It might be expected that priests and theologians, used to thinking of God as a living God, would be outraged by the suggestion that God is really present in bits of bread or drops of wine. And yet they taught that in the Mass and in the sacrament of the Eucharist, "the whole Christ is truly, really, and substantially present under both species [bread and wine] beyond the duration of the Mass, and that the presence of Christ in this manner is worthy of adoration."[1] How could they fail to see the similarity of this to idols of stone or to the ark of God that the people of Israel carried around with them and finally deposited in the permanent tent of the Temple in Jerusalem? The *Shekinah* and the ark had been associated also. But identical? I do not know how long the Church believed that this is the central mystery of the Church itself as the shrine of God. But for hundreds of years at least, the eucharistic presence, first in the Mass and then in the elements left over from the Mass, was the surest way to get close to transcendence. With the loss of faith, and change of practice, one no longer sees the old evidences of this belief in churches across the land. To go into a Catholic church today is much like a Catholic going into an Anglican church fifty years ago; it looks the same, but something is missing.

Fifty years ago—to take an undisputed figure—the remains of

the sacrament were reserved in tabernacles on altars or aumbries in walls, with a light always burning to indicate that "Christ our God" was within, waiting patiently for the humble visitations of the faithful. Parish churches, convents, and monasteries, Roman Catholic and Anglican, were open night and day for visitations: the faithful did not fail to come, falling on their knees for a few minutes, to have their daily exposure to transcendence. I dare say that for many it was the truest ontological experience of their lives, or at least they thought it was. No one else would listen and not turn away, no one else would offer full pardon. And when the tabernacle or aumbry was opened and the sacrament exposed to view in a sunburst-like holder, the faithful, on knees, singing hymns to the presence, could feel an inner transformation from supplication to adoration. *Adoro te, devote, latens deitas* (hidden deity).[2] The Lord Jesus Christ had remained "day and night in this Sacrament full of kindness and love, awaiting, inviting, and welcoming all who come to visit," believing "that thou art present in the Sacrament of the Altar."[3] And although the sacrament was sometimes fed into the mouths of the faithful, communion, except on the point of death, seemed less important than this experience of devotion.

All that has changed, at least in emphasis, since Vatican II. Biblical theology and a eucharistic theology emphasize the meal of the faithful instead of the divine sacrifice. Ontology has lost out. We no longer live in a world where adoration is more than an overcharged word. Once it was an experience accessible to the simplest of people. Sadder still, we do not really live in a world in which real communion has replaced the practice of Real Presence. We talk much about communication with people, meaning "explaining ourselves," but there is no noticeable increase in either openness or giving. Besides, there is so little to give. To give much there must be a nurturing of mystery and the infinite. If ever humankind lived near the tree of the knowledge of good and evil and not near the tree of life, it is today. That is what Kierkegaard meant when he said that we know so much, have so much information, but have forgotten what it means to exist. It would be better to know less and to imagine more.

Whoever entered a Catholic church fifty years ago, bearing marks of sickness, bereavement, guilt, or confusion of soul, knew why they were there. Those persons wanted through a few moments of intimacy with someone who would accept them, the healing mercy that only a loving parent had ever been able to give. They had been told and believed it to be true that they were kneeling in the presence of "the living Christ," "the holy mystery," "a hidden closeness, a forgiving intimacy, their real home which shares itself, something familiar which they can approach and turn to from the estrangement of their own perilous and empty life."[4] Those days are about over, and the informality of the new liturgies is not a fitting substitute for either intimacy or mystery.

Those of us who have functioned behind the scenes like the Wizard of Oz may say, "It was all a trick to fool you. There is no holy mystery, and never was. It is only bread and wine; come on in, we will show you." They may be right, but they would be mistaken if they thought it did not matter. Mystery and holiness have all but disappeared, "and we have killed him, you and I."[5] When mystery goes, the present goes also. We fulfill the prophecy of Pascal, spending our present in regret and anticipation, missing the only time we actually have, the present. Proust has been Pascal's only disciple.

It is absurd for Heidegger and Marcel, both Catholic at birth and at death, to talk of presence with such boldness as if each had discovered it. Not only have they deceived others not blessed with their religious upbringing, they omitted to tell us the sources of their familiarity with the history of the idea of presence. Presence is above all a liturgical term. If we have little idea of what is meant by supplication, thanksgiving, adoration, how can we expect to understand the source of presence as a philosophical concept? When communal opportunities for the practice of presence disappear, we cannot expect individual experiences of presence to carry the same philosophical weight.

Perhaps underneath some of the casual talk about sex these days is a secret hope that in sex we may still be able to experience the intimacy of real presence. But for most people it is probably a simulacrum at best. The mystics of the past at least understood the fullness of presence, its demands as well as its satisfactions, and, paradoxically, they made use of the language of sexual love. Too often human beings speak of one kind of experience in terms of another that they know only by hearsay.

The ground beneath presence is quicksand, its atmosphere shadowy. When I speak of the elusiveness of presence, I am not thinking only of the idea of presence and how difficult it is to define. I am thinking also about the difficulties of practicing presence, of unconditional giving. That needs two, each setting an example for the other. You cannot practice presence all by yourself. There must be a mutual dependence, an exchange. God wants our love, said Mechthild of Magdeburg. Only when we are wanted can desire expand into full presence. The ideal is one thing, the consequences of failure grim. Who knows how much may still be recovered through the wisdom of someone who believes along with Clement and Charles Williams that, "another will be in me who will suffer for me as I shall suffer for him."[6] "But first you must consent to be helped."[7]

Salve Regina

Swann's Way ends with a coda that at first reading may seem out of keeping with "Swann in Love." It ends with a paean to Woman as embodiment of the idea of perfection. This in itself would seem to be at odds with Proust's view that the only paradises are those that are lost, unless we are meant merely to assume that the Mme. Swann he shows here in the Bois de Boulogne is not the same Mme. Swann we met in "Swann in Love, " but one seen through the eyes of a boy, not a man. I suppose this is true. But the discrepancy is a little too large. Swann could never appreciate Odette's beauty, and Proust makes no effort to make us see what Swann cannot. In fact, Swann says, "To think that I've wasted years of my life, that I've longed to die, that I've experienced my greatest love, for a woman who didn't appeal to me."[8] Odette is not intelligent; her observations are banal, and she is devious. But she is real, and we can believe in her even as we despise her, even if we do not go so far as Proust as to think, "It is more reasonable to devote one's life to a woman than to postage stamps or snuff-boxes. . . . Live with a woman and you will soon cease to see any of the things that caused you to love her."[9]

Proust's treatment of other women is consistent with this. Mme. de Guermantes may be beautiful, but he does not try to convince us of that. She is known for her wit, examples of which are merely bits of cheap malice. She would not be noticed were she not the doyenne of the Faubourg St. Germain. Albertine, Marcel's mistress, has a chameleon-like face; we do not know whether she is more beautiful than anyone else, since she is chosen arbitrarily to be a permanent object of a lazy young man's manipulations. At the end of *Time Regained*, Mme. Swann, now Mme. de Forcheville, can once again be recognized as Odette. She has become the mistress of the octogenarian Duc de Guermantes. "She was so miraculous that one could not even say that she had grown young again, it was as though she had bloomed for a second time. Indeed, for me she seemed to say, not so much, 'I am the Exhibition of 1878 as I am the Allée des Acacias of 1892.' That was where, it seemed, she still might have been. And just because she had not changed, she seemed scarcely to be alive. She looked like a rose that has been sterilized."[10]

When we saw her in the coda at the end of *Swann's Way* she was another person altogether, a model for queenly beauty and elegance, indeed, a model of earthly perfection. And yet even here Proust does not lose touch altogether with reality. The Mme. Swann of the Bois is as unintelligent as ever. She has nothing to say. She smiles, she bows, she acknowledges the courtiers around her. As a person she is still thoroughly banal, but Proust by placing her in a mythical "Garden of Woman"[11] lets her reign as undisputed queen. There are no other women in this garden—she is Eve in the Garden of Eden. The translators correctly translate *Jardin des Femmes* as "Garden of Woman." Mme. Swann is Woman, and around her are all the men.

Into this paradise came also a young man "with a social longing."[12] "But it was Mme. Swann whom I wished to see."[13] And so do we as she appears on foot in a polonaise of plain cloth, a little toque on her head trimmed with a pheasant's wing, a bunch of violets in her bosom, "acknowledging with a wink the greetings of the gentlemen in carriages who raised their hats to her and said that there was never anyone so well turned out as she."[14] Later she is seen in her victoria, now "figuring for me a royal dignity, the passage of a sovereign, an impression such as no real queen has ever since been able to give me."[15] *Salve Regina*![16]

She is reclining negligently, "her hair, now blonde with one grey lock, encircled with a narrow band of flowers, usually violets, from which floated down long veils, a lilac parasol in her hand, on her lips an ambiguous smile in which I read only the benign condescension of Majesty."[17] *Mater misericordiae?* Hardly! Her lazy smile prompted men to say, "What a lovely woman!" She was dressed as people imagine queens are dressed. This woman from the demi-monde is the only satisfying model of royalty that Proust can give us. This woman "whose reputation for beauty, misconduct, and elegance was universal"[18] has almost risen out of the pages of the novel to be a presence in history. It is an extraordinary performance.

With the young narrator, the reader too may feel "an obscure desire,"[19] an "unsatisfied longing."[20] Before this fictional masterpiece of "female elegance,"[21] we may with him envisage "the idea of perfection."[22] But it is impossible to imagine him or any of her admirers saying, "*Ad te clamamus, exules filii Hevae.*"[23] At the back of my own mind I see two lines of Dominican friars, from Blackfriars, Oxford to San Domenico, Fiesole, filing down into the nave of their conventual chapels at Compline to face the altar and chant a solemn *Salve Regina.* Unlike the courtiers in the Bois they knew they were exiles.

Twenty years passed, and the narrator returns to the Bois. It is autumn, and Mme. Swann no longer appears, as she once did, "in an otter-skin coat, with a woolen cap from which stuck out two blade-like partridge feathers, a bunch of violets crushed into her bosom, whose flowering, vivid and blue against the grey sky, the freezing air, the naked boughs, had the same charming effect of using the season and the weather merely as a setting."[24] There are now motorcars instead of carriages. Worse, he himself "no longer had a belief to infuse"[25] into the people he saw. "They were just women, in whose elegance I had no faith and whose clothes seemed to me unimportant."[26] He had seen only one woman, Mme. Swann, and there will never be one like her again. It was as if he was destined to live in a time of "the death of the gods."[27]

Had Proust—or his narrator—ever found a presence in his own life that would remain faithful; if he had ever found it in him to be faithful to anyone, he would not now be celebrating nostalgia.

Mme. Swann herself was still alive. She could write him, she could tell him about the past. He would see her at the Princesse de Guermantes'. But the real women whom he now saw were "no more than grim spectres of what they had once been, wandering, desperately searching for heaven knew what, through Virgilian groves."[28] The Bois was no longer "the Elysian Garden of Woman."[29] The sky was now gray, the wind wrinkled the surface of the Grand Lac, birds flew over with shrill cries. The forest was vacant and deconsecrated. "How paradoxical to seek in reality for the pictures that are stored in one's memory. . . . The reality that I had known no longer existed."[30]

How paradoxical to search in memory for any kind of reality when reality is still with us. Reality is more than "a thin slice, held between contiguous impressions that composed our life at that time."[31] Reality is people and places, and the bonds between people; it is "houses, roads, avenues,"[32] all "fugitive, alas, as the years."[33] It is all we have: the immediacy of the real. Nostalgia and an ideal of perfection are substitutes for this. *Mater amoris* has become a substitute for *Mater misericordiae*. It is when we lose hold on reality that we dream of some perfection to take its place, and it fails us in the end, as it failed Proust.

Viaticum

According to Nietzsche, Epicurus once said, "If there are gods, they do not care for us." A biblical theologian would say, "If they do not care for us, they are not God." The God of the Bible lives and cares. That is what is meant by "presence," and it is the reason the Bible uses anthropomorphic and personal imagery to suggest the reality of God. God is not an ideal, but a real presence in the world.

Proust was no believer, and he disavowed firsthand knowledge of shared love. His fiction gives us no example of reciprocity of presence, even though it contains notable examples of the kind of love that human beings have looked to God for. Not only is the narrator blessed by the loving-kindness of his mother and his grandmother, there are moments when he experienced in his affair with Albertine a tenderness that reminds him of real love. Only there, and not in the long unhappy love of Swann for Odette, is there any hint that Proust knew that love and sexuality may share a common ground.

What is different about Albertine? Who is she? "She is legion. . . . The truth is that this woman has merely raised to life by a sort of magic countless elements of tenderness existing in us already in a fragmentary state."[34] Would this not be true of any love affair at the beginning? Her whole life filled him with desire, the desire of penetrating another life. To a curiosity about the unknown had been added a sensual desire.[35] He had dreamed as much when he saw the milk-girl at the halt on the way to Balbec. When he says that "Albertine was beginning to inspire in me a desire for happiness,"[36] he had in mind shared affection and tenderness as well as sensual desire.

If we have had trouble remembering Albertine, as opposed to Odette, it may be that we have been given too many Albertines to remember. Perhaps she should seem to us all the more real for that. She is real enough; we know chameleon-like people, but she is not yet a presence. We do not usually remember Albertine except as The Girl—as Odette was The Woman. And all that the narrator has already told us of Swann's jealousy, he now repeats when writing of Albertine. Except for one thing: Albertine is a figure in two scenes of comic misunderstanding, unimaginable with Swann and Odette.

When Marcel first met her in Balbec, she invited him to call on her at night in her bedroom, where a Stendhalian scene was enacted when Albertine pulled the bell rope to prevent Marcel from kissing her. As he bent over her, supposing that she wanted to be kissed, he thinks, "Death might have struck me down in that moment and it would have seemed to me a trivial, or rather an impossible thing, for life was not outside me but in me. I should have smiled pityingly had a philosopher then expressed the idea that some day, even some distant day, I should have to die."[37] He fancies that he was "about to discover the fragrance, the flavour which this strange pink fruit concealed."[38] Then he hears the bell.

She never refused him anything again. Poor girl that she was, she hoped to capture him as a husband; by becoming his captive she lost whatever mystery she had had for him. Before kissing her for the first time he thought, "I should have liked, before kissing her, to be able to breathe into her anew the mystery which she had had for me on the beach before I knew her. . . . I am going to discover the fragrance of the secret rose that blooms in Albertine's cheeks."[39] He speculates on the function of lips, and describes what he sees as his lips came near her face. "Suddenly my eyes ceased to see, then my nose, crushed by the collision, no longer perceived any odour, and, without thereby gaining any clearer idea of the taste of the rose of my desire, I learned from these obnoxious signs that at last I was in the act of kissing Albertine's cheek."[40] No longer a mystery, no longer a person either, just a cheek. So much for immediacy.

But Proust knew more than that; he knew something about sexual intimacy. And it is only when he writes of Albertine the captive that he comes near writing about the presence of a woman with a man. When he sees her asleep, he recovers his faculty of dreaming, dreaming of "the possibility of love."[41] At such times he "felt a love as pure, as immaterial, as mysterious, as if I had been in the presence of those inanimate creatures which are the beauties of nature."[42] He thought then that he would never tire of her, for she was "within my reach something as serene, as sensually delicious as those nights of full moon on the bay of Balbec."[43] Their love had not yet reached the point when he would have to say, "My hell was the whole region of Balbec."[44] Indeed, he would get in bed with her and caress her while she slept. But he still knew that he could not "penetrate into the depths of her being."[45] Only asleep could Albertine persuade him that time could stop, and with it his own poisonous suspicions and jealousy.

At other times Marcel waited for her to come to him in his bed. In the darkness lighted by the glow of the fireplace, their caresses were blind but more tender than usual. In his arms Albertine seemed to say, "Do what you like with me,"[46] while she gave him "incomparable kisses of peace."[47] "She used to slide her tongue between my lips like a portion of daily bread, a nourishing food that had the almost sacred character of all flesh upon which the sufferings that we have endured on its account have come in time to confer a sort of spiritual grace."[48] When she slipped her tongue in his mouth, he felt that she was "making me the gift of the Holy Ghost, conveyed to me a *viaticum*, left me with a provision of tranquility almost as precious as when my mother in the evening at Combray used to lay her lips upon my forehead."[49] We too recall that he had said of that time that his mother "had bent her loving face down over my head, and held it out to me like a host for an act of peace-giving communion in which my lips might imbibe her real presence."[50]

As the mystic uses the imagery of human love, so now Proust uses the imagery of divine love. Eros and agape are interchanged. The viaticum, gift for a dying man on his last great journey, is like the real presence of the Eucharist, a thanksgiving for the gift of love. Compared to something Plotinus once said, Proust does not come off badly. Plotinus believed that only in the world beyond this one does the real object of our love exist. "Anyone who has had this experience will know what I am talking about. The soul lives another life as it advances toward the One, reaches it, and shares with it. Thus restored the soul recognizes the presence of the dispenser of the true life."[51] For Proust's Marcel, Albertine is the dispenser of true life, and his description of her presence to Marcel is as real as anyone else could say. Even his own "impure love for Albertine"[52] was blended with "the tender charm of an affection at once filial and maternal."[53] He recalls "that immense heart"[54] of his grandmother, and "the radiance of her tender love,"[55] and his dream of her after her death when he was "filled with an unknown divine presence."[56]

Of course, Albertine is not a divine presence. She is too inarticulate to be a human presence. And yet before dismissing the eroticism of Proust, we should ask whether we should not also dismiss the erotic lyrics of the Song of Songs. When Marcel opened her chemise to see her uplifted breasts and "the junction of her thighs closed by two valves with a curve as languid, as reposeful, as cloistral as that of a horizon after the sun has set,"[57] he stops thinking of himself long enough to cry, "O mighty attitudes of Man and Woman, in which there seeks to be united, in the innocence of the world's first days and with the humility of clay, what the Creation made separate!"[58] Proust, however, would have had to change his character not to immediately remind himself that "the amorous life [is] the most precarious of all, that in which the unpredictable rain of suphur and brimstone falls after the most radiant moments,"[59] and that "at the heart of their intimacy there lurks a painful disquiet."[60] After all, like the rest of us, he is speaking out of a human condition "after this our exile."[61] Even so, he confessed that, "It is precisely because this tenderness has been necessary to give birth to pain—and will return moreover at intervals to calm it—that men can be sincere with each other and with themselves when they pride themselves on a woman's lovingness."[62] All that is missing is a complementary lovingness on the part of a man. What he experienced with Albertine was different, "something that had hitherto been foreign to my amorous existence, if it was not entirely new to my life. It was a soothing power the like of which I had not experienced since the evenings at Combray long ago when my mother, stooping over my bed, brought me repose in a kiss."[63]

Once again it can be said that Proust has secularized religious imagery. Or is it possible that that is the only imagery that tells the truth about what it is like to live on the threshhold of presence? He has made it real by telling the truth; he has told the truth by making it real. Language and experience together prove our tenative maneuvering on that threshhold. C. S. Lewis closed his fable *Till We Have Faces* with lines that could have been used by Proust. "I know now, Lord, why you utter no answer. You are yourself the answer. Before your face questions die away. What other answer would suffice? Only words, words."[64] Proust's answer is not just words, but the faces of his mother, his grandmother, and his mistress Albertine. What other answer would suffice?

Postscript

In the West we still have an almost insuperable inclination to separate the religious from the secular. Even those for whom "blasphemy" is a dead word may think it poor taste to place visiting the Blessed Sacrament side by side with a night with Albertine: "Now my tongue the mystery telling, of the glorious body sing,"[65] alongside a paean to the body of Marcel's captive mistress. Many of us are Manichees in spite of our sophistication. We accept the divorce of feelings that just as feelings cannot be told apart. We elevate the purity of devotion to what may well be abstraction, above the undeniably sensuous adoration of what can be touched.

But the ontological experience—if that is what it really is, and not just a pretending—of the Eucharist can be less Christian than the attachment of man to woman as celebration in the Song of Songs. Who can offer a devotion to the Blessed Sacrament that can match the considerateness of one person for another? It still is more blessed to give than to receive.

There are different practices of presence, and not necessarily one love. Is it really more than words to say, in prayer, that one offers oneself to God? Unless one means that one is just repudiating life. To withhold oneself is not by any means the same as giving oneself (to God or anyone else). Worship can be extraordinarily self-centered and indifferent to the reality, let alone needs, of others. And so can love of another person, a child, a spouse, a lover. The intensity of longing in Song of Songs is equally applicable to adoration of God or another human being. But longing is not a test of presence, unless it is marked at the same time by a considerateness that attempts to break through to the real truth of the being one longs for. By itself longing is only a function of loneliness, that hollowed-out feeling of isolation from reality. And loneliness cannot be relieved by longing, only by the reaching out of someone present.

Western attitudes toward love and sex—especially Christian—are still corrupted by a kind of manichean dualism. We have not yet taken in what should be perfectly obvious, that human beings are indivisible. We are not body *and* mind, body *and* soul, flesh *and* spirit: we are body-soul, body-mind, flesh-spirit. And yet we have the strange capacity to think and behave as if we are divided. This is one reason why expressions of presence are so unsatisfactory and unstable. We are not always sure whether longing is of the mind or of the body. And so we have sex without love and prescribe love without sex. Is it any wonder that we are less than human when we practice the first, and half-creatures of the night when we prescribe the second? Who can tell how it was in the dim past when we read of men and women more charged up than most of us now? And yet even today the most moving occasions for the practice of presence in this vale of tears are to be found in the fullness of love-sex between human beings, the longing and the fulfillment of flesh-spirit. Instinctively the saints knew this, and that is why Song of

Songs has been the principal literary paradigm for all love poetry. The truth, I think, is that this paradigm worked because it was saying something that even the least poetic of human beings recognized as real. The saints just said it better, and Song of Songs was their model. The vocabulary belonged to them, but the experience belongs to all of us, if we are lucky. There is much of luck in the practice of presence. Never again must there be eros without agape, or agape without eros, if, with luck and common sense, we can avoid it. Let us celebrate whole men and whole women from here on.

Longing is evidence of the beginning of love, not a manifestation of love's fullness. Glory is a manifestation of presence, but not its surest manifestation. Presence can sink under the weight of glory, just as charm can divert attention from kindness. Only a living presence that listens with its whole being to another whole being can transform loneliness into union. The weight of such listening is truly glorious. Constancy is that weight.

NOTES

1. Josef Andreas Jungmann, in *Encyclopedia of Theology*, ed. Rahner, 455.
2. Hymn of St. Thomas Aquinas.
3. Prayer of St. Aloysius Liguori, in *Manual of Prayers*.
4. Rahner, *Foundations of Christian Faith*, 131.
5. Nietzsche, *The Joyful Wisdom*, par. 125.
6. Clement, in Williams, *Descent of the Dove*, 37.
7. Williams, *Descent into Hell*.
8. Proust, I, 415.
9. Proust, *The Guermantes Way*, II, (vol. 6, p. 58, Chatto & Windus ed.).
10. Proust, III, 993.
11. Proust, I, 452.
12. Proust, I, 452.
13. Proust, I, 453.
14. Proust, I, 454.
15. Proust, I, 453.
16. Compline Hymn from *Manual of Prayers*.
17. Proust, I, 454.
18. Proust, I, 455.
19. Proust, I, 458.
20. Proust, I, 458.
21. Proust, I, 459.

22. Proust, I, 459.
23. "To thee we cry, exiled children of Eve."
24. Proust, I, 461.
25. Proust, I, 460.
26. Proust, I, 460.
27. Proust, I, 460.
28. Proust, I, 462.
29. Proust, I, 462.
30. Proust, I, 462.
31. Proust, I, 462.
32. Proust, I, 462.
33. Proust, I, 467.
34. Proust, III, 513.
35. Proust, III, 499.
36. Proust, II, 810.
37. Proust, I, 995.
38. Proust, I, 995.
39. Proust, II, 377.
40. Proust, II, 379.
41. Proust, III, 64.
42. Proust, III, 64.
43. Proust, III, 65.
44. Proust, III, 528–29.
45. Proust, III, 67.
46. Proust, III, 72.
47. Proust, III, 72.
48. Proust, III, 2.
49. Proust, III, 72.
50. Proust, I, 14.
51. *The Essential Plotinus*, 86.
52. Proust, III, 73.
53. Proust, III, 73.
54. Proust, I, 718.
55. Proust, I, 718.
56. Proust, II, 783.
57. Proust, III, 74.
58. Proust, III, 74.
59. Proust, III, 75.
60. Proust, III, 75.
61. "Salve Regina," in *Manual of Prayers*.
62. Proust, III, 75.
63. Proust, III, 71.
64. Lewis, *Till We Have Faces*, 269.
65. Hymn of St. Thomas Aquinas.

A
Secret
Understanding

Not everything can be said easily, except claims of absolute affirmation or denial. In time most things can be said clearly, at least. And some of these things are so important that we should do everything we can to make them clear. Presence is one of these things. It is not a word that we should allow anyone to rule out of our vocabulary and discourse.

It may not be possible to work out a theory of presence that can meet all the objections of either philosophy or criticism. Perhaps one should not even try, at least until the objectors show more familiarity with the phenomena of presence than have been shown here. One cannot please everyone anyway, and should not be bullied into trying. It is safer—more neutral—to try to call to mind "the imperious radiance of sheer presence,"[1] wherever it can be felt or found.

I should be neglecting the main sources of appropriate illustration if I did not call on both religion and metaphysics when I try to tell the story of the idea of presence. It will not go unnoticed that the presences that they record look very like the encounters of persons with persons that are familiar to most of us already. We know that the language of metaphysics and religion (particularly mystical religion) is to a large extent interchangeable with the language of human love.

It is one thing to question whether when philosophers talk of Being they really know for sure what they are talking about; it is another to doubt that they have something in mind that they can-

119

not say in some other way. When we listen to great mystics talking about experiences with God, it is not necessary to decide whether they were deluding themselves; it is only necessary to admit that they were saying something that could not be said in another way. For all that, it is a fact that, Being and God aside, the rest of their terminology and the main patterns of their thinking are strikingly similar to the patterns of thought we use when we are thinking about ourselves and each other. This is why I am impatient with both Heidegger and Marcel: there was a larger intellectual context for their insights, both religious and secular, than either acknowledged. Whether the mind is working with metaphysical or mystical or psychological language, the issue remains the same: what is "the end of man,"[2] as the medieval philosophers would say? What is the ideal pattern of life, and idea, the experience for which one can live and die? Is there an idea that will let us expand our hold on reality, confirming our capability of taking in what is real in our lives? On the few occasions when philosophers and literary critics have considered the idea of presence, they have been inhibited by supposing they were looking for something perfect instead of something possible or appropriate.

Granted that it is probably not possible to know anything or anyone completely. For me it has been enough to recall Augustine's sayings, "Man is a great deep," and "We are dark to each other, dark to ourselves." Therefore, we must speak of what we can know, not of what we would like to know. Granted also that the question about presence raises the issue of whether we can know anything or anyone in any degree of immediacy. For me, it is enough to remember Proust's own accounts of time as if stopped, his many little apprehensions of fragments of life. They suggest presence, and for me suggestions come pretty close to proof. I am thinking not only of his revelatory flashes of sense perception—like the episode of the madeleine—but longer tales, such as sunrise on the train to Balbec. What one should be looking for are phenomena that are luminous, just as a theologian looks for evidence of the numinous in encounters of men and women with God.

Presence is elusive—one cannot say this too often—just as the very soul of a person is elusive. Thinking about either presence or the soul is extremely difficult and seldom satisfies unless presented in story form. Even then it may elude understanding. Stories carry more verisimilitude than analysis. We can marshal claims and definitions to try to reflect intuitions of what is real, but the intuitions themselves must arise from living experience. Moments, meetings, persons are our verification. In the stillness of being with someone else, we may touch on something that gives a sense of something great we have been waiting for. This is what happened to the young man on the train at sunrise when he saw the milk girl approach up the slope. Proust was wiser than most of us are. He did not confuse dream with reality. He knew that boy and girl came from different worlds that they could never share. But he also knew that it is very important to seize moments that expand our awareness of what we would like to be.

There is no presence without some kind of encounter. Presence is never a strictly solitary experience, not even our presence to ourselves. That is why it is necessary to give some attention to both biblical thought and mysticism. Many others have gone our way before us. So many had encounters with something or other that they were convinced was real and more lasting than time and space. It is just not possible to dismiss everyone who is different from ourselves as deluded. Some of them were quite as sophisticated as we. And they knew that the phenomena of presence are, as Buber said, "strange, lyric, and dramatic episodes, seductive and magical, tearing us away to dangerous extremes, shattering security."[3] Buber was not thinking primarily of theophanies either. He was simply acknowledging that if real life is a meeting, it is likely to be an uncomfortable meeting. Whoever is tempted to think Moses and Jacob had comfortable fireside chats with the *Mysterium Tremendum*[4] has not read very carefully or is depending on tepid experience. The women ecstatics, Christian or Sufi, who fantasized about their desperate love affairs with God knew more about passion than did their secular contemporaries. I say this partly because it is to them, not their secular contemporaries or our own, that we go when we look for information about love. They make us, with all our manuals on sex, look emotionally deprived. This is what I have in mind when I say that presence is an ideal, and an ideal that some strange people such as Mechthild of Magdeburg or Rabia may already have realized.

It is not unreasonable also to point out that biblical and mystical encounters or the passion of Heloise for Abelard or Heathcliff for Cathy Earnshaw have a similar shape, and that the language of presence applies to them all. And we can find affirmations in the metaphysicians, Heidegger and Marcel, for example, who seem to be talking about the same inner world that we run across in literature. Buber was right when he insisted that while we must not spend our lives in passionate meetings—there is much else to do—in the end it is presence of some sort that will decide whether we are fully human. It is always possible to lose our soul by not understanding this. It happens every day.

The philosophers and theologians I have mentioned all knew what I do about the narrative shape of presence; they were as well read as the best of us. But maybe they should have remembered more of what they had read. And Proust, who was so sure he himself was incapable of presence as to doubt that anyone else is either, may have known more than fitted this theories. Gabriel Marcel favored a new kind of metaphysics, more phenomenological we might say, a "concrete" or sensual metaphysics. But I say, better take Proust's "two Ways," the Méséglise Way and the Guermantes Way, relate them to metaphysical desire and you will have a concrete metaphysics.

Is this romantic? Of course. If there is such a thing as a romantic theology, that is, the theology found in novels, so there can be a romantic metaphysics, metaphysics found in stories. Take, for example, the story of Augustine with his mother in Ostia, "leaning from a window which overlooked the garden in the courtyard of the house where they were staying. . . . There we talked together, she and I, in deep joy . . . and while we were talking of His Wisdom and panting for it, with all the effort of our heart we did for one instant touch it."[5] They shared what Alain-Fournier called "a secret understanding,"[6] an understanding of what life is really like. This is presence, where neither space nor time matters momentarily, and where there are no questions, doubts, or anxieties, only quiet and light. It is the shape of nirvana, the shape of the dark contemplation of John of the Cross, the mutual identification of Cathy and Heathcliff, a shared understanding.

This is the secret understanding that François Seurel had with his best friend's wife. We know what it was like because we know how that friend, Augustin Meaulnes, felt when he first saw the spire of the turret of the Sand-Pit Manor through the fir trees, and later sat in the drawing room of the manor listening to Yvonne de Galais play the piano. What Meaulnes felt, what Seurel understood, was a vision of what life could be like: "an emotion he could not have defined, an extraordinary sense of well-being, an almost intoxicating serenity, the certitude that the goal was in sight, and that he had nothing but happiness to look forward to."[7] It is Alain-Fournier speaking, but it might be St. Augustine or Mechthild of Magdeburg or John of the Cross, or even Proust. This is "the secret understanding that only death was to bring to an end,"[8] and it is the source of love's constancy.

And yet, as *Le Grand Meaulnes* demonstrates, there is no joy that cannot be renounced, no adventure that cannot fail. Presence is always at risk, and the real enemies are the ones that can be avoided. Buber again was right when he insisted that we cannot seek presence (although we can long for it); it must be taken, or we must be taken, by surprise. It can, however, be lost by negligence. Presence is not a utopian experience. It cannot erase all distance or death, but one can live as if it could. Presence is more than something felt; it must be something shared, where neither space nor time is a final category. This is something Immanuel Kant did not know.

Presence suggests an alternate way of thinking about time and space, especially time, as a filled present instead of as something recovered from the past by memory. Pascal's warning has scarcely been heeded. "We never keep to the present. . . . We anticipate the future as if we found it too slow in coming and were trying to hurry it up, or we recall the past as if to stay its too rapid flight. We are so unwise that we wander about in times that do not belong to us, and do not think of the only one that does. Thus we never actually live, but hope to live."[9] A joy that is related to something gone forever is quite different from a joy in the presence of something seen or someone loved. "In your presence is the fullness of joy."[10] Proust may have been right to think that if there is no such thing as presence, then life is one disappointment and deception after another, anguish unlimited. He thought he knew a way around that, by drawing his consolation from involuntary memory. What was solace for him may be only more anguish for us. Proust did not believe in real presence, but he had a pretty good idea of what it would be like if one could have it. We have to go beyond Proust, beyond his intimations of mystery in the experiences he did know. Proust at least knew the difference between an ideal and an illusion. He knew that if you can touch presence, it is real. We need witnesses who have touched it.

This is what is suggested also at the end of the Gospels, and especially in the meeting of Jesus and Mary at the empty tomb. Mary, weeping, says, "They have taken away my Lord, and I don't know where they have laid him." As she said this she turned and saw Jesus standing there, though she did not recognize him. Jesus said, "Woman, why are you weeping? Who are you looking for?" And she, supposing him to be a gardener, said, "If you have taken him away, tell me where you have put him, and I will go and remove him." Jesus said, "Mary!" She then knew him and said in Hebrew, "Rabboni" or Master. Jesus said, "Do not cling to me, because I have not yet ascended to the Father."[11]

When Jesus said her name, he unlocked the door to her soul, her secret understanding with him. All the other resurrection scenes are stories about presence that are meant to suggest the overcoming of loss, betrayal, and death. Mary had shared with Jesus his dream of life that he knew from his experience with his Father. She had learned from being near him what real living was meant to be. Her tenderness reached out to his radiance. Like all the others who had followed him, she wanted a reassurance that she was not ultimately alone. When she and the other disciples found it, it was as if for the first time.

We have gone beyond suggestions of obscure desires and obscure pleasures, however special they may seem. We have even gone beyond metaphysical desire which is not always very particular about what can satisfy it. A sense of presence is never as satisfying as presence itself. Feeling may be a place to start from, but it is not a place to end. Only a shared life built on shared dreams and shared understanding, and on shared pain, can begin to get the demons back into Pandora's box. This is the hope of presence. Real presence is more than a hope and a struggle. It is, as C. S. Lewis said of his sense of his wife's presence after her death, "just intelligence and attention."[12] It is a phenomenon to be treasured for itself. Real presence is the end of humankind.

A Final Unscientific Postscript

Existential thinking should include the complete range of the phenomena of both consciousness and personal experience. But the existentialism of Augustine, Pascal, Kierkegaard, Jaspers, and Heidegger has for the most part been limited to aspects of crisis: the "boundary-situations" of struggle, suffering, guilt, decision, death (to which I would add a spectrum of identity: disquietude, loneliness, search for the secret self, being in love, failure, rejection, time running out). These represent the darker side of life and are inescapable. I have always believed that existential thinking should admit another side as well, call it what you may: nostalgia, promise, moments of grace. This is not meant to be offered as a theoretical observation only. As one nears the end of one's life, the pressure to record something worth saying is terribly strong, strong enough even to try to write a book like this.

Presence is both an ideal and a reality. When we say that someone is a presence or has presence, we mean that he or she seems to be giving him- or herself, even imposing himself or herself. And we feel we are in the presence of a whole someone. This is part illusion, I admit, for no one is whole until dead, and no one, however much he or she tries, can reveal or give all of the self. Compared to the self at other moments, or compared to others who are shut off from us, we do think of some as more open, more whole, than others. Indeed, we sometimes feel we are in the presence of someone qualitatively different from others, and we remember their quality long after they have gone from us. They affect us differently from those who are closed to us. With them and through them we seem to leave the subject-object world of epistemology and penetrate a land of participation, acceptance, understanding. Nevertheless, strictly speaking, presence is always an approximation of our longing for an end to barriers.

Similarly, there are times when time itself seems to stop for a while and we no longer feel the conflict within us of memory and desire and the fragmented busyness of what we call the present.

Neither past nor future disappears completely; they are but waiting in the wings. But we have some experience of what it would be like if we could live permanently in the stillness of a now. Of course we cannot, and we are imagining an ideal not recording a reality. Except for one thing, the comparison with the rest of our time when consciousness struggles incessantly with all three phases of time at once. What a blessed relief and pleasure to leave that behind. We do not really experience the present time by itself; but we almost do. So presence, whether as a function of knowledge or a function of time, is virtual, an illusion strictly speaking, but powerful nonetheless. Presence is always to some extent a phenomenon of "as if." The immediacy of the relationship between persons, the simplification of time present are two sides of the same instinct man has for ideal reality. The degree to which each of us is able to approximate this ideal will determine the value of our lives.

Let us begin again. What do we mean when we think of presence? I should like to be able to reply, "We think of what it is like to be alive." And so it is, if one forgets momentarily the "boundary-situations." It is to remember that life is unpredictable, persons are unpredictable, we ourselves are unpredictable, and that sometimes personal relations are both mysterious and miraculous. It is to know that sometimes there are experiences that for a little while lessen the dread of separation, loneliness, and even death. We are never safe, but within experience itself we are justified in dreaming of what life would be like if we were. We would know as we are known and be the simple wholes that we have failed to be.

The metaphysician uses the same language, out of desperation, as the mystic; and the mystic uses the same language as the man or woman in love. They speak of intimacy and use its terms. There are different motives and different reaches of consciousness that propel people toward metaphysics and mysticism and sex, but the pattern of intimacy is much the same in all three, even though the intentions seem different. When the metaphysician and theologian speak of the closeness of Being or God to the human mind, they are thinking of the ease and grace of sharing, accepting, understanding. It is the same for each of us in the presence of someone who is willing to take us as we are and who offers himself or herself in return.

This is an experience well-known within families, and in friendships, teaching, healing.

One who has experienced presence may indulge himself by saying things such as, "Presence is where there is no longer space, only time, no longer past, only present, no longer fear of the future, only a dream of the future." Or, "Presence is where there are no more questions, only answers." Very well, let us indulge ourselves for a moment with dream and radiance. There will be plenty of time yet for questions about presence as possibility and presence as reality, questions on the difference between actuality and dream or illusion, between the virtual and the usual. The minds of those represented in this book had a toughness that can stand up well to any skepticism. We ought to respect them for what they know and what they show. They may yet persuade some to take a new look at possibilities never considered seriously before. It is not too late to reverse pre-judgments and to look beyond intellectual fads. It is never too late to start all over, and that can be exciting. Human beings really do have some talent for surprising and exceeding themselves.

NOTES

1. Steiner, *Real Presences*, 122.
2. Thomas Aquinas, *Summa Contra Gentiles*, Bk. III.
3. Buber, *I and Thou*, 34.
4. Otto, *The Idea of the Holy*, iv.
5. Augustine, *Confessions*, Bk. IV, 10.
6. Alain-Fournier, *Le Grand Meaulnes*, 138.
7. Alain-Fournier, *Le Grand Meaulnes*, 48.
8. Alain-Fournier, *Le Grand Meaulnes*, 138.
9. Pascal, *Pensées*.
10. Ps. 16:11.
11. John 20.
12. Lewis, *A Grief Observed*, 57.

Selected Bibliography

Alain-Fournier (pseud.). *Le Grand Meaulnes.* New York: Penguin Books, 1982.

Aquinas, Thomas. *Selected Writings of Thomas Aquinas.* Edited by M. C. D'Arcy. New York: Everyman, 1940.

———. *Summa Contra Gentiles.* New York: Random House, 1945.

———. *Summa Theologica.* New York: Random House, 1945.

———. *Theological Texts.* Edited by Thomas Gilby. London: Oxford University Press, 1955.

Arberry, A. J.. *Sufism.* New York: Penguin Books, 1970.

Augustine. *Confessions.* Translated by R. S. Pine-Coffin. New York: Penguin Books, 1979.

———. *An Augustine Synthesis.* Edited by Erich Przywara. New York: Harper, 1958.

Barth, Karl. *Epistle to the Romans.* London: Oxford University Press, 1977.

Bernanos, Georges. *Diary of a Country Priest.* New York: Doubleday, 1974.

Book of Common Prayer, with the Psalter. New York: Seabury, 1953.

Bronte, Emily. *Wuthering Heights.* New York: Penguin Books, 1965.

Buber, Martin. *I and Thou.* Translated by Ronald Gregor Smith. New York: Scribner's, 1958.

———. *At the Turning Point.* New York: Farrar, Straus, 1952.

Cloud of Unknowing. (anonymous). London: Burns & Oates, 1960.

Dionysius the Areopagite. *The Mystical Theology.* London: S.P.C.K., 1957.

Dostoevsky, Fyodor. *The Idiot.* Translated by David Magarschack. London: Penguin Books, 1955.

Eckhart, Meister. *Selected Writings.* Translated by James M. Clark and John V. Skinner. London: Faber & Faber, 1958.

———. *Meister Eckhart: A Modern Translation.* Translated by Raymond Bernard Blakney. New York: Harper, 1957.

_____. *An Anthology of Sermons.* Translated by James M. Clark. London: Thomas Nelson, 1957.

Eliade, Mircea. *Yoga.* Princeton: Princeton University Press, 1971.

Gregory of Nyssa. *From Glory to Glory.* Translated by Herbert Musurillo. New York: Scribner's, 1961.

Griffiths, Bede. *The Marriage of East and West.* London: Collins, 1985.

Harper, Ralph. *The Existential Experience.* Baltimore: Johns Hopkins University Press, 1972.

_____. *The Sleeping Beauty and Other Essays.* Cambridge: Cowley Publications, 1985.

_____. "The Return Journey: Some Theses on the Ontological Imagination." *MLN* 97, no. 5 (December 1982), Johns Hopkins University.

Heidegger, Martin. *Being and Time.* New York: Harper, 1962.

_____. *Existence and Being.* Chicago: Regnery, 1949.

_____. *Introduction to Metaphysics.* New Haven: Yale University Press, 1973.

_____. *On Time and Being.* New York: Harper, 1972.

_____. *Sein und Zeit.* Halle: Niemeyer, 1935.

_____. *Early Greek Thinking.* New York: Harper, 1975.

Hemingway, Ernest. *A Farewell to Arms.* New York: Scribner's, 1957.

Hilton, Walter. *The Ladder of Perfection.* London: Penguin Books, 1957.

Homer. *The Iliad.* Translated by Richmond Lattimore. Chicago: University of Chicago Press, 1962.

Hopkins, Gerard Manley. *Poems and Prose.* London: Penguin Books, 1962.

James, Henry. *The Complete Notebooks.* New York: Oxford University Press, 1987.

James, William. *The Varieties of Religious Experience.* New York: New American Library, 1958.

Jaspers, Karl. *Philosophy.* Vol. 2. Chicago: University of Chicago Press, 1970.

Jerusalem Bible. New York: Doubleday, 1966.

John of the Cross. *Collected Works.* New York: Doubleday, 1964.

Kafka, Franz. *The Castle.* New York: Schocken, 1974.

_____. *The Trial.* New York: Schocken, 1974.

Kierkegaard, Søren. *Concluding Unscientific Postscript.* Princeton: Princeton University Press, 1941.

_____. *Journals.* New York: Oxford University Press, 1951.

King James translation of the Holy Bible. Cambridge.

Kundera, Milan. *The Unbearable Lightness of Being.* New York: Harper & Row, 1984.

Lavelle, Louis. *La Présence Totale.* Paris: Aubier, 1932.

Letters of Abelard and Heloise. Baltimore: Penguin Books, 1974.

The Life of St. Teresa of Avila. London: Penguin, 1957.

Lewis, C. S. *A Grief Observed.* Greenwich, Conn.: Seabury, 1963.

_____. *Till We Have Faces.* New York: Time, 1966.

_____. *The Lion, the Witch, and the Wardrobe*. London: Geoffrey Bless.

_____. *The Weight of Glory*. London: S.P.C.K., 1954.

Loyola, Ignatius. *Spiritual Exercises*. Westminster, Md.: Newman, 1957.

Malcolm, Norman. *Ludwig Wittgenstein, A Memoir*. New York: Oxford University Press, 1966.

Mann, Thomas. *The Magic Mountain*. New York: Alfred A. Knopf, 1952.

The Manual of Prayers, Authorized by the Hierarchies of England and Wales. London: Burns, Oates & Washbourne, 1953.

Marcel, Gabriel. *Being and Having*. London: Dacre, 1949.

_____. *Homo Viator*. New York: Harper, 1962.

_____. *The Mystery of Being*. London: Harvill, 1950.

_____. *The Philosophy of Existence*. London: Harvill, 1954.

Maréchal, Joseph. *Studies in the Psychology of the Mystics*. Albany, N.Y.: Magi, 1964.

Mechthild of Magdeburg. In *Soul Afire*, edited by H. A. Reinhold. New York: Pantheon, 1944.

Mehta, Ved. "Personal History." *The New Yorker*, December 19, 1988.

Nietzsche, Friedrich W. *The Joyful Wisdom*. London: T. N. Foulis, 1910.

Novum Testamentum Graece. Cambridge: Oxford University Press, 1944.

Otto, Rudolf. *The Idea of the Holy*. London: Oxford University Press, 1952.

_____. *Mysticism East and West*. New York: Macmillan, 1972.

Painter, George. *Marcel Proust: A Biography*. London: Chatto & Windus, 1971.

Pascal, Blaise. *Pensées*. New York: Dutton, 1954.

de' Pazzi, Maddalena. In *Soul Afire*, edited by H. A. Reinhold. New York: Pantheon, 1944.

Plotinus. *The Essential Plotinus*. Translated by Elmer O'Brien. New York: New American Library, 1964.

Proust, Marcel. *A la recherche du temps perdu*. Pleiade edition. Paris: Gallimard, 1954.

_____. *Remembrance of Things Past*. 3 volumes. Translated by C. K. Scott Moncrieff and Terence Kilmartin. New York: Random House, 1981.
Vol. 1: *Swann's Way, Within a Budding Grove* (cited as Proust I)
Vol. 2: *The Guermantes' Way, Cities of the Plain* (cited as Proust II)
Vol. 3: *The Captive, The Fugitive, Time Regained* (cited as Proust III)

_____. *Remembrance of Things Past*. 12 volumes. Translated by C. K. Scott Moncrieff. London: Chatto & Windus, 1971.

_____. *Selected Letters, 1880–1903*. Edited by Philip Kolb. Chicago: University of Chicago Press, 1988.

_____. *Marcel Proust: A Selection from His Miscellaneous Writings*. London: Wingate, 1948.

Rahner, Karl. *Foundations of Christian Faith*. New York: Crossroad, 1984.

_____, ed. *Encyclopedia of Theology*. New York: Crossroad, 1975.

Rolle, Richard. *The Fire of Love*. London: Penguin, 1972.

Schillebeeckx, Edward. *Jesus*. New York: Crossroad, 1979.

Scholem, Gershom. *Jewish Mysticism*. New York: Schocken, 1941.

Shah, Idries. *The Sufis*. New York: Doubleday, 1971.

Steiner, George. *Real Presences*. London: Faber & Faber, 1989.

Tillich, Paul. *The Courage to Be*. New Haven: Yale University Press, 1952.

_____. *Systematic Theology*. Volume 1. Chicago: University of Chicago Press, 1951.

Unamuno, Miguel de. *The Tragic Sense of Life*. Dover, 1954.

Underhill, Evelyn. *Mysticism*. New York: Dutton, 1961.

_____. *Worship*. New York: Harper, 1937.

Williams, Charles. *The Descent of the Dove*. New York: Meridian, 1956.

_____. *He Came Down from Heaven*. London: Faber & Faber, 1950.

_____. *Descent into Hell*. London: Faber & Faber, 1937.

Wittgenstein, Ludwig. *Tractatus Logico-Philosophicus*. London: Routledge & Kegan Paul, 1966.

Zaehner, R. C. *Hindu and Muslim Mysticism*. New York: Schocken, 1969.

Proust – Vol. I, 15 – "sense of her real presence"

When your absence is fresh and new, when I can say, "Yesterday he was alive...."

(Jesse Murry died yesterday, Jan. 13, 1993.

You are so recently dead, so lately alive